Rec. by Phyllis

Praise for *Farewell*

D0499131

"A chuckle or a wry grin is waiting on [...] of humor that builds gradually, that [...] stealth that you hardly even realize what a good time you're having. By the end of *Farewell, My Subaru* you can think of nothing that would seem like more fun than hanging out at Fine's ranch, vainly striving to keep his goats from eating the rose bushes. Think James Herriot's *All Creatures Great and Small*—updated for the iPod generation."   —*Salon*

"Fine is Bryson funny."   —*Santa Cruz Sentinel*

"[Fine] set himself the goal of living 'off the grid' for twelve months. The results were hilarious as well as enlightening: nearly electrocuting himself with solar panels, fueling his truck with waste oil from a local Chinese restaurant, and learning to live with coyotes, goats, and an eclectic assortment of neighbors."   —nationalgeographic.com

"Changing the way we live is not a single decision but a learning process, and *Farewell, My Subaru* makes clear that process can be a challenge—and a hoot."   —*St. Petersburg Times*

"An instructive, fascinating and often hilarious account of one man's efforts to embark on a 'hypocrisy reduction project' and get back to nature . . . an entertaining book . . . It constitutes a powerful antidote for the apathy and defeatism that for too long have haunted our thinking about the environment and the future."   —*Portland Tribune*

"For those readers who are actively trying to reduce their carbon footprint, this book will reinforce their knowledge and offer ideas and firsthand experience. For those who have an emerging awareness of these issues, it will be a humorous, informative source. Above all, promoting the formation of acommunity economies is a critical lesson to teach the next generation."   —fredericksburg.com

"Mr. Fine is a very funny man. . . . His adventures in green Digital Age living will keep you howling and wondering what bizarre thing is going to happen next." —*Tucson Weekly*

"The details of Doug Fine's experiment in green living are great fun—but more important is the spirit, the dawning understanding that living in connection to something more tangible than a computer mouse is what we were built for. It'll make you want to move!" —BILL McKIBBEN, author of *Deep Economy: The Wealth of Communities and the Durable Future*

"Fine isn't exactly Mr. Green—as he readily admits, he's never grown so much as a single tree or, for that matter, used any farming or ranching utensils. In the end, that's perhaps what makes his story so appealing—and, more important, believable: After all, if a guy like this can milk his own goats and grow his own peas, shouldn't we all? Fine's easygoing writing style and humor will keep you engaged through the end."
                                                        —treehugger.com

"Even covering foreign war zones wasn't enough to prepare Doug Fine for a fossil-fuel-light life at the remote Funky Butte Ranch in Southern New Mexico. Near electrocution installing solar panels, floods and a hen-munching coyote named Dick Cheney are all detailed in rollicking fashion in *Farewell, My Subaru*."
                                                  —*The Santa Fe New Mexican*

"A funny and inspiring story. Doug Fine, who 'grew up on concrete pizza' in American suburbia, [writes of] his attempts to kick oil while still living like an American in a small farm in New Mexico . . . Nothing like a good story about experiencing green living with a self-deprecating sense of humor."
                                                        —ecolibris.net

"Fine's funny struggle to become a better world citizen will entertain both the eco-aware and those who doze peacefully in their home's formaldehyde fumes."
                                                        —BookPage

FAREWELL,
MY SUBARU

ALSO BY DOUG FINE

Not Really an Alaskan Mountain Man

FAREWELL, MY SUBARU

AN EPIC
ADVENTURE
IN LOCAL
LIVING

———

DOUG FINE

VILLARD ⓥ NEW YORK

To protect privacy, some human names and dates have been changed.
The names of members of most other species are real.

2009 Villard Books Trade Paperback Edition

Copyright © 2008 by Doug Fine

All rights reserved.

Published in the United States by Villard Books, an imprint of The Random
House Publishing Group, a division of Random House, Inc., New York.

VILLARD and "V" CIRCLED Design are registered
trademarks of Random House, Inc.

Originally published in hardcover in the United States by Villard Books, an imprint of
The Random House Publishing Group, a division of Random House, Inc.; in 2008.

Valisa's Kung Pao Chicken with Cold Sesame Noodles
recipe on page 90 comes from http://lekkertje.blogspot.com.
Grilled Rattlesnake Dijon recipe on page 123 comes from
http://www.ces.ncsu.edu/martin/wildrecipes/wgrratt5.htm.
Potato, Pepper, and Onion Frittata recipe on page 153 comes from
http://foodblogga.blogspot.com.

As of press time, the URLs displayed in this book link or refer to existing
websites on the Internet. Random House, Inc., is not responsible for the
content available on any such site (including, without limitation, outdated,
inaccurate, or incomplete information).

LIBRARY OF CONGRESS CATALOGING-IN-PUBLICATION DATA

Fine, Doug.
Farewell, my Subaru : an epic adventure in local living / Doug Fine.
p.   cm.
ISBN 978-0-8129-7789-9
1.   Fine, Doug.   2.   Environmentalism—New Mexico—Biography.
3.   Sustainable living—New Mexico—Biography.   4.   Human ecology—New
Mexico—Biography.   5.   Green movement—New Mexico.   I. Title.
GE198.N45.F56 2008
333.72092—dc22   2007042533

Printed in the United States of America

www.villard.com

2   4   6   8   9   7   5   3   1

Book design by Jessica Shatan Heslin/Studio Shatan, Inc.

For Sally McGuire,
who, in asking me to housesit
one fateful week in the
early twenty-first century,
allowed me to discover
my affinity for the goat mind

In three minutes, 98 percent of all the matter there is or will ever be has been produced. We have a universe. It is a place of the most wondrous and gratifying possibility, and beautiful, too. And it was all done in about the time it takes to make a sandwich.

—BILL BRYSON,
A Short History of Nearly Everything

If something's hard to do, then it's not worth doing.

—HOMER J. SIMPSON

CONTENTS

PART FOUR: SOLARIZED

PART FIVE: GROWTH

PART ONE

———————

DROUGHT

I want to put a ding
in the universe.
—STEVE JOBS

ONE

THE PARKING

BRAKE

WAKE-UP

CALL

As I watched my Subaru Legacy slide backward toward my new ranch's studio outbuilding, the thought crossed my mind that if it kept going—and I didn't see why it wouldn't—at least I would be using less gasoline. A few days after I moved into the sprawling, crumbling, forty-one acre New Mexico spread that I had named the Funky Butte Ranch (it had a funky limestone butte on its east side where two great horned owls with an active love life nested), I neglected to firmly apply that last click to the parking brake on my aged fossil fuel–powered hatchback, the LOVEsubee.

This was a good thing. Really. The imminent demise of my

ride, I rationalized, would help me with one of my four big goals for the next year, which were:

1. Use a lot less oil

2. Power my life by renewable energy

3. Eat as locally as possible

4. Don't starve, electrocute myself, get eaten by the local mountain lions, get shot by my UN-fearing neighbors, or otherwise die in a way that would cause embarrassment if the obituary writer did his or her research

Epiphany in the desert Southwest is not subtle. Almost nothing in this stark, gorgeous ecosystem is. I moved several thousand miles from my place of birth in order to kick fossil fuels and live locally. Three days later, MY CAR WAS LITER-ALLY RUNNING AWAY FROM ME. This is how lessons are taught in a place where even sitting down means a possible impaling. I figured I would forge success from astonishing, seemingly irrevocable defeat, you know, like Al Gore.

I didn't need the message hammered home so literally. The time was absolutely right for me personally to embark on this adventure in living green—other than having no electrical, plumbing, building, engine mechanical, horticultural, or animal husbandry skills at all, that is. After growing up on Dominoes Pizza in the New York suburbs, at age thirty-six I wanted to see if a regular guy who enjoyed his comforts could maintain them with a reduced-oil footprint. In concrete terms, this meant raising animals and crops for my food, figuring out some way besides unleaded to get anywhere, and making bank account–draining investments in solar power.

I'd lived and worked in extreme conditions on five continents since the beginning of my career as a journalist fifteen years ago, but time and again, after shivering in Alaska and dodging bullets in Tajikistan, I reaffirmed what I already knew: I like my Netflix, wireless e-mail, and booming subwoofers. In fact, I didn't want to live without them. I just wanted to power them by the sun. If my ear-melting music could go solar, and still make my UN-fearing neighbors complain about bass lines interrupting their nightmares of Hillary Clinton, I'd consider this experiment a success. If I had reliable Internet and could download movies into my green world to boot, the feeling would be closer to "Eureka!" Especially if I was eating munchies I'd grown, raised, or at least bought locally.

It takes three to four years of powering your home to offset the energy used to make your solar panels.

Because as I saw things, global climate change, pollution, world wars, and human rights aside, the Oil Age has had a great run: fossil fuels turned the United States, for example, from a nation of farmers into the Jetsons. I largely welcome this. I know I sure dig my laptop. When else in history could I have listened to Malian drumming or Beatles outtakes (or some DJ mixing the two) all within three clicks? When else could I *be* that DJ? This really is the best time ever to be alive, if you're fortunate enough to live in the West and not be in the armed forces. In short, I wanted to prove that green Digital Age living was possible, and I was psyched to get cracking.

Coincidentally, society seemed to be ready, too, or at least to have transformed from considering such an experiment radically subversive to simply radically unfeasible. By 2005, when I moved to New Mexico, even a marginally coherent man deemed president of the United States was struggling to pronounce "biofuels" at the State of the Union Address. Citigroup, the world's largest company, announced in 2007 that it was investing $50 billion in green projects. Companies were marketing everything from "sustainable" mascara to green SUVs. What was next? Environmentally friendly gunpowder? Organic Raid roach spray? Nothing would surprise me at this point.

From Zambian government officials (who refused genetically modified organism seeds during a recent famine) to Russian spies (who continued to kill one another over their boss's natural gas policy), it just felt like a critical mass had recognized that the fossil fuel–powered civilization that got us to this point was in big trouble. Maybe it has fifty years, maybe one hundred left in its life cycle. In addition to my personal reasons, to my "environmentally sensitive while comfortable" motivations, I saw adaptation as a matter of survival.

I didn't know if the current green rage was just another trend—a fad until oil prices came down a little. But what if $2.29 gas prices weren't coming back? What if $3.29 oil prices weren't coming back? What started out as a cute whim for me quickly became a much more personal journey.

Whether I needed the lesson or not, the LOVEsubee was gathering a head of steam. I recall the instant I discovered that I had a parking brake issue on my hands. Perhaps three quarters of a second earlier, halfway between my car and house, I caught the hint of something moving in my peripheral vision. I had just returned from what would become my weekly, monumental supply run to the town of Silver City, twenty-three miles away. In my possession were five store-bought, organic, box-ripened tomatoes, "grown" eight hundred miles away in California and shipped to the crunchy Silver City co-op via roughly a hundred twenty gallons of fossil fuels.

Life had been idyllic for a brief moment that July afternoon. Two green Rufous hummingbirds ignored FAA altitude requirements around my head, and I had an unfamiliar proprietary sense about them and everything on the ranch. I was going to be here for a while, and there was evidence everywhere. For instance, I had already bought an actual non–thrift store bed. An expensive, four-figure one, following an extensive test in the furniture showroom that nearly got me evicted from the store. For a thousand bucks, I thought the mattress should hold up to every kind of rigor.

The Funky Butte Ranch being the first property I had ever owned, I was kind of sauntering through the postclosing honeymoon phase in a haze of bliss, excessive capital outflow, and plans. In fact, I don't know why they call that nightmare at the title company a "closing." It should be called an "opening."

An opening to new projects, loves, entire worldviews. I found I was already becoming much more of a fiscal conservative, now that I owed property taxes for the first time. Small government suddenly seemed the way to go.

Alone on my new property, my mind was also wandering. Wandering in the way a healthy guy's mind wanders when he's got time to think—and not just because of all the mattress testing. I was freshly single again, after a long and spiritually unsatisfying relationship. My body was still adjusting. In my first few days at the Funky Butte Ranch, in fact, I kept censoring conversations between my pituitary and my cerebrum that went along these lines:

PITUITARY: *Why don't we take a little break from repairing the goat pen to find out if the ol' Sweetheart wants to take a little break from whatever she's doing?*

CEREBRUM: *The ol' ex-Sweetheart isn't in our life anymore. She lives in a McMansion two hundred fifty miles away.*

PITUITARY: *Fine. I'm sure you can provide a substitute.*

CEREBRUM: *Look, we can't bring home the goats and get started on this local living project if we don't secure the goat pen from predators. Did you not see the mountain lion teeth marks on that deer carcass in the creek bed? There are other things in life besides sex.*

PITUITARY: *You think so? Try and think about anything else while you're working on that cow pen.*

CEREBRUM: *Goat pen.*

PITUITARY: *Whatever.*

But there was no time for daydreaming. I turned my head and there it was, my car of twelve years (and crash pad from time to time), gliding furiously in reverse, and, it should be pointed out, not on fossil fuels, across my irises and down the hill toward the beautiful stone building I planned to use as a writing and dance studio. It all happened so fast. Before I even had time to say "Come back, LOVEsubee!" a one-hundred-year-old live oak, like a last defender on a long kickoff run-back, knocked the vehicle off its trajectory. It miraculously came to rest against a ten-foot yucca, a variety featuring spears that would suffice for medieval combat.

"Firmly apply the parking brake" is the message I was getting as I moronically waved my vine of nonlocal tomatoes at the LOVEsubee. "To your unsustainable life. To petroleum in your very food and coal in your hot water. To relationships based on lust. The whole thing."

As a person raised on the East Coast of the United States, I bring a healthy skepticism to anything that sounds too Whoo Whoo (and New Mexico is perhaps the World Capital of Whoo Whoo gurus, diets, left- and right-wing conspiracies, and alien sightings). But I couldn't even park my car at my new ranch without the world screaming "Less Oil. More Heart."

TWO

A LAND

LIKE

MATZO

My friend Lacy, a tobacco-chewing, ponytailed, New Age–inclined lifelong New Mexican, came right over with a come-along (a sort of a chain and winch good for Extreme Leverage), as he always does when I screw up, and we extracted the LOVEsubee in an hour-long battle with gravity.

"What exactly are you planning here?" he shouted during the effort.

"I'm trying to show that a regular American can still live like a regular American, only on far fewer fossil fuels," I screamed out of the LOVEsubee window.

"Can you say that again?" Lacy asked amid a cloud of fossil fuel smoke. "I can't hear you over the revving engine."

It was late July in the midst of the longest drought since the last Ice Age, so we were only three quarters of the way toward terminal dehydration when the LOVEsubee, sporting an oak antenna garland and an impressive armor of yucca spines, coughed back up to the dirt parking area below the Butte. It looked like a stegosaurus.

I looked vaguely reptilian myself, from all the scuffling with the local plant life. But there was a trade-off for this nerve-rattling mayhem. I saw immediately that the Parking Brake Incident had cleared an absolutely perfect spot to plant my herb garden: it was shaded by the oak, close to the main house, and, now, plowed and tilled by a Japanese All-Wheel Drive Vehicle with 204,000 miles on it.

A few days later, I sunk some leeks, cilantro, basil, lettuce, and rainbow chard in the ground and decided I felt pretty good about the Subaru slide. I was already starting to live locally, a crucial and unsung component of reducing oil use. Once the first sprouts started poking up, I decided I couldn't have manufactured a better start on the Funky Butte Ranch.

Eating local food is something that had appealed to me since well before I learned how many troughs of jet fuel it takes to get even an organic banana from Honduras to New Mexico. Forget about the petroleum-based fertilizers that go into the "commercially grown" avocadoes from California. Or what the farm workers are (or are not) paid in both places.

I like fresh, local food because fresh, local food tastes better than fake, factory-produced food. It's a quirk in my taste buds. I was born with this obstreperous belief that food should taste good. I was thought of as a "bad eater" as a kid because I could wait out my whole family at the dinner table in a stand-off over a charcoal briquette being billed as "steak." Actually, I was and remain a great eater of actual food. Luckily, I have the metabolism of a hummingbird and the exercise regimen of a cheetah.

Food that has to travel not only tastes funky, it often doesn't even look right. I vividly recall one afternoon trying to squeeze a baseball of a tomato in a Long Island, New York, supermarket at about age nine. It wouldn't budge. I tried bashing it against the ground, lobbing it at a passing shopping cart, and even jumping on it. Before my mom cuffed my ear, I had created the merest slit near the object's equator. It was the start of my career as a careful label-reader.

> The average tomato travels fifteen hundred miles from the field to the table.

ENTICING TOMATO BASIL SNACK

Hunk of goat cheese or fresh mozzarella, thinly sliced
2 home-grown, vine-ripened, organic tomatoes, sliced
6 home-grown basil leaves
6 stone-ground sesame crackers
Pinch salt

Place (bottom to top) cheese, tomatoes, and basil on crackers. Top with hint of salt. Put Frank Sinatra or Bill Evans Trio on the stereo. If enjoying with a romantic partner, be sure to have sufficient birth control on hand prior to eating.

Since I've begun growing tomatoes myself, I know that no matter what I try, from baking by my giant south window to long watering neglect during travel, they come off the vine succulent and almost overpoweringly delicious. You have to genetically modify a "tomato" in order to make it that much of a rock. Which is exactly the intent: attractively orange but impossibly durable fruit doesn't get damaged during shipping from distant hothouses. It's all about the Monsanto stock price.

I think it should be all about the taste, and the nutrition. In that order. But it's hypocritical of me to act as though I'd been a total Conscientious Objector to the Oil Age. My own attempts at living green before moving to New Mexico were far from pure. Even during a stint in rural Alaska, when I was all proud of myself for catching and canning a year's worth of salmon, I did it by buzzing around with a nasty two-stroke outboard engine. I could see the gas and oil seeping out into the pristine waters where the salmon swam. By the time I got to the Funky Butte Ranch, I was dedicated to exploring if I could really live green and local, with a minimum of hypocrisy. Even if, say, gas stations and Wal-Marts went away.

> Every year, the average American adds four tons of carbon dioxide to the atmosphere based on food choices alone.

But I also knew that even if I wanted to, I couldn't completely cut out petroleum and Chinese slave factory products, not in the first year or two of the project. They were too entrenched in my life. How would I toast my bagels? And I'm sorry, but even in my most remote years as a journalist, I remained pretty attached to toilet paper. It was in my life nearly every day. Oh, and most of all, ice cream. No matter what happens to society, I must maintain my supply of ice cream. This is my secret primary reason for raising rambunctious goats.

Still, I thought I could gather some momentum in the effort during my first year, enough to feel whether it was possible, whether I was firmly on the way to independent, local, oil-reduced survival or doomed to the fate of those, like most of my family and friends still, who believe that the current McGlobal Economy is eternal. Most of us who enjoy the comforts of Western culture hold fast to this belief. Unlike any society that came before, we'll figure out a way to keep this Super Bowl–watching, espresso-drinking, GPS-guided-car-driving party going no matter what the ice caps, a couple of Jihadists, the petroleum engineers, and some nasty microbes in the Hot Zone have to say. It's the societal equivalent of not thinking about dying.

I don't like to think about dying, either. But if I had stopped to look at my overall survival ability when I embarked on this experiment, I concede that it would look like I had a death wish. Without any of the skill sets that allowed earlier pioneers to eke out a life here, I chose New Mexico for the project, both because I love the mellow culture and vast wilderness, and because I thought it would have some of the best solar power potential on the planet.

Extremely hot weather actually makes solar panels operate less efficiently—you get about 0.5 percent less production for every degree centigrade increase in temperature.

Sure, I had to drive across the dry beds of the Mimbres River (a mile away, between me and the nearest paved road) and Stitzel Creek (on my property) to even access the canyon that contained my nine-hundred-square-foot, thirty-year-old adobe composite home. But heck, locals said it'd been two years since a major flash flood. Sure, the land resembled matzo, and barring a massive climactic shift that included sudden deluges of rainfall, I'd have to corral my own milk goats for a couple of years until the range recovered from previous mules on the property.

I was OK with all that. The one thing life as a roving journalist teaches you is that there's no point bitching about the weather. I donned the inexplicable regional hat, bought me the ranch, and started integrating words like "I reckon" and "bought me" into my vocabulary.

Global warming might even be a boon to my project, I thought upon move-in and all the associated perspiration. When it comes to solar power, New Mexico is in fact the place to be. Passive Heat Gain, which sounds like a mental disorder associated with menopause, has been utilized by the local adobe culture for at least a thousand years. Today, New Mexicans of every gender, political inclination, and cultural background stop me on the street when they see a solar panel in my truck and insist on shooting the breeze about their theories on wattage, placement, and current inversion. It's like the way Chicagoans know about wind, or Angelinos about traffic.

Solar panels are mandatory on all buildings in Spain.

There was certainly enough sun here for even a neophyte solar aspirant. I recall Raoul, the owner of the glass store in Silver City, a rapidly crunchifying, hip little town of ten thousand where Billy the Kid was once imprisoned, telling me not to sweat the positioning of the solar water collector I was surrounding with two panes of his finest tempered glass (delivered via fossil fuels and made through God-knows-what polluting process—so much for a minimum of hypocrisy).

"Man," he said, sounding a lot like Cheech. "There's enough sunlight here from all directions. It's almost sunny at night."

Indeed, I detected a decided absence of moisture in the New Mexican air. I mean to say, there was none. The world was drier than a Steven Wright monologue. I didn't mind this one bit. I love the sun. I spent my first New Mexico afternoon runs greeting neighbors with a wonder-filled, "Isn't it a *beautiful* day?"

They sort of looked at me with an expression that said, "Um, every day's a beautiful day here, son."

In fact, when I switched off my iPod and asked my gazillionth-generation neighbor Señor Mendosa for his take on the drought while I was trespassing on his ranch during a run, he didn't tell me climate change is changing everything in his crops and orchards. He told me it already *has* changed everything.

"There hasn't been a normal rainy season for ten years," the silver-haired elder told me as he tilled his corn. "We never had anything like this weather when I was growing up. Neither did my father. Or his father."

> The number of reports of hail and severe wind in the United States have gone up tenfold in the past fifty years.

News reports promised more of the same for about, oh, about the next three thousand years. The cover of the latest *Farmer's Almanac* (and can I say how proud I was that I needed a *Farmer's Almanac*?) screamed, "Watch out! Another wild year ahead." Indeed, around the time of my closing/opening, there was some talk of shutting the highway to town, on account of half the nearby Gila National Forest being on fire. I could smell it on my runs.

It wasn't just the forest that was suffering. A biologist came by to check out the recently healthy but now deceased deer that had been providing take-out buffet for the local coyotes, wild cats and vultures since a couple of days before I moved into the Funky Butte Ranch. It fell about sixty yards from the studio the LOVEsubee had barely avoided. The scientist told me that he was unsure if the deer had been killed by a mountain lion or had dropped dead from sheer thirst.

> If the Greenland ice sheet melts entirely, sea levels would rise twenty-three feet, flooding out hundreds of millions of people and inundating cities like New York, London, and Shanghai.

I was glad the predators had a distraction from the goats I was soon to pick up from my Craigslist seller in Tucson. And frankly, I was glad they had a distraction from me. Before I found the Funky Butte Ranch, I had rented a wasp-infested one-room straw bale shack about four miles farther up this valley, which is called the Mimbres, after the river. When friends visited, they would insist on going to the outhouse armed with a two-way radio, merely because I had been stalked by a mountain lion once or twice and because there were tracks all over the place. I don't know what they expected to convey to me upon an attack: "Breaker, Breaker. I'm being eaten while reading the latest issue of the *Home Power Magazine*. Over."

The point, though, is that everyone and everything in New Mexico was thirsty, and when I moved to the Funky Butte Ranch, it was making creatures, which I would personally have "forgotten" to load on Noah's Ark, pay me visits, like the two toilet-exploring scorpions I nearly sat on on my second night at the ranch.

THREE

LAST EXIT

TO

WAL-MART

The evening after Lacy helped me extract the LOVEsubee from the putative herb garden, I watched the sunset from the peak of the Funky Butte with my new Australian cattle puppy, Sadie. It took about ten minutes to scale it. I couldn't believe I "owned" nearly everything I could see.

Home.

At only 6.1 percent interest.

Still, home. One of the platoon of Realtors I'd worked with in finding this spot talked about the "Pyramid of Self," with home space at the absolute base. "Once you've got that," she said. "You can build almost anything else you need in your life."

I took a moment to reflect on this. As a wandering journalist who had spent two decades crashing on couches from the Arctic to Rwanda, her words resonated deeply. I could now shop for more than two days of food at a time. Or better yet, I could try to grow a year's worth. If my solar power and local ranching plans came to fruition, maybe I really *could* live a truly independent life, right from here. It seemed doable.

A solar-powered airplane flew for fifty-four straight hours over New Mexico in 2007.

But until then, I realized, I was hopelessly dependent not just on co-op veggies, but on Silver City's one box store: a Super Wal-Mart the size of a small state. I didn't like to think about it, but the LOVEsubee's hatch was filled with one of those giant Val-U pyramids of paper towels that looked as though the trees had simply been converted from living, bark-covered plants to dioxin-bleached rolls of about the same girth and height.

In fact, on that same town run that netted me the oil-soaked organic tomatoes, I had pulled into the vast Wal-Mart parking lot seeking a water bucket for my new goats. It was an ugly reality: here I was, trying to live this local, healthy life, and my parts list was coming from China. The lifestyle contrast was too stark to ignore. I had a bag of organic goat grain in the LOVEsubee, for crying out loud. I was at a crossroads: was I going to go green and independent, or was I going to keep the Walton family buying Picassos? Shopping locally was an important part of my effort, and I knew it.

Trade with China accounts for more than half the U.S.'
$850 billion trade deficit.

But it was hard to avoid Wal-Mart in rural America at the dawn of the twenty-first century. In fact, I hit the Wallyworld exit every time I went to town. It was open all the time, and its crappy, slave-made junk was often cheaper than the crappy, slave-made junk at the town's local stores. There was always some excuse to head there ("online shopping also involves oil miles," "the local stores don't carry fly strips"), and progressives in my part of New Mexico were all too aware of the dilemma.

A product imported from Shanghai travels 6,438 miles
to get to a market in Los Angeles. There were
7.2 billion visits made to Wal-Mart in 2006. Earth's
population is 6.5 billion.

"Busted!" we said to each other, jabbing the other guilty party in the ribs when we found friends in the gardening or paper towel aisle.

So as I did every week, earlier that day I had parked and trekked across a fire zone slightly larger than Namibia, returned the cheerfully fake greeting from the front-door shoplift guard, and lowered my sunglasses for protection from the bolt of sickly fluorescent light that pelted me when I entered the store that was laid out exactly the same as thousands of sister spore properties all over the planet. Even the temperature and humidity were regulated from Arkansas. The place was like a garden of discount retail soil that cultivated an ever-increasing crop of desperate shoppers. It even fed and watered them. In a sense, Wal-Mart executives could be considered farmers.

Shopping at Wallyworld invariably got out of hand. I thought I just needed paper towels and a bucket, and wound up investing in tire polish, mops, marbles, and roofing. There was no such thing as using the express lane. Plus, I almost never escaped without a genuine Wal-Mart preroasted rotisserie chicken. These came in lemon-pepper, barbecue, and "traditional" (traditionally preroasted?) flavors. The chickens, about the size of large hamsters, were cheap, and provided sustenance for three days to busy journalists.

On this visit, I had noticed that there was a "price rollback" on small pumps (one supplier in the Philippines had obviously undersold another in Indonesia), and it made me think about this arid region I was settling into. Water pumps (originally windmills) are the reason people are able to inhabit the Mimbres Valley. The Mimbrenos, the local folks who were here before the Americans, the Spanish, and the Apache, took off for Mexico the last time the climate acted this funky, leaving behind only their gorgeously psychedelic pottery filled with beans I intended to plant on the Funky Butte Ranch.

The original Mimbrenos, in fact, were one of my sources of optimism about my own chance to thrive in southwest New Mexico. Before they disappeared, leaving the thirteenth-century equivalent of the oven on, the members of this indigenous culture were so successful in my very valley that healthy adults were known to live well into their thirties. I took a lot of comfort from the Mimbreno pottery shards that were scattered all over the region, including some flints on the Funky Butte Ranch. That people did well here long before Wal-Mart I found encouraging. Standing in the toxic hardware and plastic bucket aisle, I thought that all the Mimbrenos needed were some well pumps and we might still be carving petroglyphs and using clay goat water buckets.

But the Mimbrenos didn't have pumps, so now we shopped at Wal-Mart for water buckets made from petrochemicals. But did we have to? Looking around me, I saw that the place wasn't hurting for business. Where did these people come from? Was I way outside the mainstream to even think about local living? I knew that the region's water tables, even with pumps, were in danger from the growing population of my patch of desert near the NAFTA-porous Mexican border. Despite our distance from Santa Fe and Taos, we already had enough Californicators seeking dream houses to ensure that mine is the first county in history where a majority of the population are Realtors. At the moment, most of the new arrivals seemed to be seeking discount bedding.

Nearly 20 million commercial trucks were registered in the United States in 1997. These vehicles drove more than 420 billion miles and consumed more than 42 billion gallons of fuel.

I decided that day, right beside the marked-down Mariah Carey CD bin, to begin to wean myself from the McMega store. It wasn't going to be easy. There were just so many situations that demanded the kind of product in which Wal-Mart specializes.

Take, say, pet carriers. About a week earlier, just as I was preparing to move to the Funky Butte Ranch, I had rescued a stray cat named Robin, one of the world's great mice-slaughterers, who went into heat the day after I brought her home. Every tomcat in New Mexico was suddenly prowling the perimeter of my straw bale rental house. This prompted an emergency town run.

Using those nails that had overnight decimated the local rodent population, Robin had managed to claw her way out of the computer box in which I was transporting her. I noticed this when I found a small distressed cat on the back of my neck about thirteen miles into my drive to town. I veered wildly, clawing blindly at her and giving thanks for the sparse back-road traffic.

After the operations (Robin's ovaries and my neck), I asked the vet staff what I should do to get the groggy cat home.

"See if you can get a carrier," the receptionist suggested.

"But where can I get a pet carrier in Silver City on a Tuesday evening?"

She didn't hesitate. "Wal-Mart."

"There's no other option?"

"Not that I can think of."

What the hell was I going to do? I don't know what the Mimbrenos did for pet carriers ("What would the Mimbrenos do?"
being a question I tried to ask myself in many of my lifestyle
quagmires). I reckon I could've performed the cat spaying myself. But on reflection I didn't own any anesthesia.

Seven hours after my vow to avoid box-store shopping, I sat
atop the Funky Butte in a semi-lotus, with ubiquitous Sharp
Desert Stuff turning me into one of those bed-of-nails
swamis. With Arkansan chicken still in my belly, my thoughts
moved through the day's events at the Funky Butte Ranch. The
runaway LOVEsubee. A new herb garden.

Suddenly a firm resolve hit me. I had been doing things
half-baked; conducting my relationships, catching salmon,
shopping for dry goods. I wanted to do things fully baked. No,
wait, that didn't come out right. What I meant was I was going
to dive into this experiment with everything I had. Although I
didn't realize how literal that "dive in" pledge would soon
prove. I would do it one project at a time. Maybe after a year,
I'd see some real reduction in the oil in my life. But it wouldn't
be a cakewalk. At the moment, even with solar panels, I would
survive as long as crunchy co-ops imported tomatoes and box
stores provided preroasted protein.

I was done making resolutions for the day, so I stood up and
pulled various stickers and Chinese star burrs out of my flesh.

I noticed I was panting. Since it was after dark, the temperature had dipped back into the high two digits. I watched a smear of stars materialize. It soon became so dense that I could barely make out individual suns. I realized that most folks in these light-blinded days don't even realize how populated our galaxy is. A coyote yipped not far off. Sadie left off munching some dry gramma grass and snapped her head around to sniff out her canine cousin.

I started to scramble down the Butte back to the ranch house and a tomato-and-basil cracker. I took a huge hit of dry night air—the desert evening is one of heaven's great blessings—and to my shock lightning in the distance winked back at me. Wait a second. Were those clouds on the northern horizon? I rubbed my eyes in disbelief, then amusement. How quaint and odd. I felt like an Eskimo kid looking at his first pineapple.

I didn't give the incoming front much thought. I had a ranch to turn clean, green, and local. This meant a million plans and tasks and objectives, all geared to one end. There were solar panels to order, biofuels to investigate, contractors to beg to work me into their "schedules." Most important, I had goats to pick up, deworm, hoof-trim, and feed twice a day. Since icky factory chicken was still working its way through me, it was easy to make local protein my first priority on the Funky Butte Ranch. That, I hoped, would keep me from the Wal-Mart rotisserie.

I was almost dizzy with the awareness of how much work was ahead of me, so when I got back inside I fired up the grid-powered subwoofer. I proceeded to dance for hours to the

tranciest beats I could find on my iPod, the way a college stu-
dent shrugs and goes out for a beer when faced with too much
studying. In between songs, I remembered that I'd bumped
into my valley neighbor Sandy Jones at the co-op earlier in the
day. She was a local environmental heroine who had lived
pretty independently for three decades while trying to inform
the world about what the area copper mining operations were
doing to the groundwater. She didn't exactly rev me up about
my chances of success when she told me, "You're doing this
alone? (*Guffaw*) You've got yourself into a two-person project.
What you need, boy, is a wife."

PART TWO

———

FLOODED

Turn Around, Don't Drown.
—New Mexico State public service pamphlet
advising against driving across flooded rivers,
found in a drawer on the Funky Butte Ranch
upon move-in.

FOUR

LIVESTOCK SHOPPING IN THE DIGITAL AGE

I can't explicitly prove that the New Mexico Realtor Association was engaged in a conspiracy with the National Weather Service, so I'll just leave it as coincidence that the most serious August flood in recorded history chose to begin less than a week after I bought a property that required two water crossings to access the rest of the world. The once-annual desert-monsoon season had simply waited seven years to arrive almost the moment I moved in.

I left the Funky Butte Ranch in what I thought was a freak thunderstorm, and it was still raining when I returned home with two baby goats from a Craigslist pickup in Tucson. Or I should say when I tried to return home. The whole landscape had saturated in the two days I was gone and now looked more like an ocean than the Chihuahuan desert. This was a problem. I needed to cross the Mimbres River in order to make the last mile to the Funky Butte Ranch.

> Even in an arid desert, it is possible to live off harvested rainwater (http://www.harvestingrainwater.com/).

The goats sounded ready to be home, too. Their backseat driving, once we hit the spine-rattling New Mexico dirt roads, took on a harmony of complaint evocative of a slaughterhouse. I tried singing "Homeward Bound" to them, which seemed to quiet them a notch. But it didn't look at all sure that we would get much farther homeward. I couldn't help observing that the river, ankle-deep when I left, was now in the Class Three range. There were rapids. Whitewater crested midchannel. Uprooted cottonwood trunks were cruising downstream like alligators late for lunch.

I parked at the bank in a steady drizzle and flipped open my cell phone. I didn't know that Janice, my goat saleswoman, was expecting a customer service call so soon. But as I stepped out of the LOVEsubee into almost elastically mushy, knee-deep mud, I was pretty sure I needed advice from a goat guru.

"How important is it that the baby goats get to a safe, dry home space tonight?" I asked Janice.

"Dry?" she said. "Are you planning on getting them wet?"

"Well, I hope not to. But I'm looking at the Mimbres River here, and I'd call it fifty-fifty if we'll make it across." My foot made a sucking noise as I pulled it out of the ground that was the consistency of pudding.

"They *do* need someplace safe to sleep," Janice said. "They could get stressed and sick if they stay cooped up in the car too long."

But that would be marginally better than drowning, right? I thought. Into the phone, I said, "Hang on, I'm gonna go out and test the depth. It doesn't look *too* bad."

"Don't do that!" Janice yelled from Arizona. "People die that way *all the time*."

It was true. I had just read about this exact phenomenon in a Louis L'Amour western. Flash floods can surge in a matter of seconds. L'Amour called greenhorn ranchers like me "rawhide" operations, as in "*an outfit that's held together with rawhide, otherwise it would fall apart.*" Nonetheless, I put the phone down on the LOVEsubee hood and edged into the water, a modern pioneer with two goats and a goat guru screaming at me.

The air and water were both still warm despite the late hour, and the world smelled not just like rain, but like a lot of rain. But, oh, the river felt lovely climbing over my sandals. A soothing massage after all that desert driving. I sloshed onward into the current. In two steps it had reached my ankles. Then my calves. The river peaked at my thighs midchannel, about the height at the top of the LOVEsubee's tires.

I turned around and skipped the thirty feet back to dry land. "I'm gonna go for it," I said into the cell.

"Oh jeez." Janice sighed. How many potential repeat customers had she lost to ill-advised flood crossings? "Call me if you . . . *when* you make it across."

Taking her self-edit as a vote of confidence, I pushed the zaftig alfalfa hay bale I had strapped to the roof of the LOVEsubee onto the ground and covered it with a tarp. It easily weighed a hundred forty pounds, and I thought it might be better to lighten my load as much as possible for the crossing. I jettisoned all kinds of junk from my Tucson shopping spree as well, stashing them under a tree near my neighbor's "UN Free Zone" sign. I wondered what he would make of my Wal-Mart exposé DVD. He'd probably call the sheriff.

OK. Enough delay. Now was the time for action—especially since the river was rising by the minute. Had it done nothing but rain while I was gone? I studied the current. I had done some guiding in Alaska, so I was trained to "read" rivers. True, most of this training surrounded travel in actual river rafts, but I figured the same principles applied to car crossings. Mulling my choices from the driver's seat, I opted for the "going as fast as I can will get me across faster" method. This meant that I left foot-deep tire tracks in the mud moments before the LOVEsubee hit the river and went briefly vertical as the goats loudly wondered, "Do we not have *any* say in who adopts us?"

That was the last time a motorized vehicle would successfully make it across the Mimbres River for a month and a half. That is, if you consider a river-soaked engine block and a dislocated wheel bearing evidence of a "successful" crossing. I do, considering that three days later my neighbor Jake flipped his monster truck midchannel, escaping through his sky-side window while his vehicle, now a boat, floated toward nearby Mexico. Still, I wasn't too proud of myself, since I had foolishly left the driver-side window open as my goats and I rafted across the Mimbres in a Subaru, and twenty gallons of liquid New Mexico and one small fish had landed in my lap.

Was it only five hours ago that I got the goats? I wonder what any witness must have thought that wilting August afternoon in Tucson, watching a well-groomed thirty-ish woman transfer two tiny, snot-dripping animals with huge, floppy ears from her truck to a Subaru hatchback, while a shaggy guy in a straw cowboy hat passed her a check. Was there some sort of kinky trade in goat parts gaining popularity at Arizona house parties?

I was twenty minutes late for the two p.m. goat pickup because I'd been rushing around to Whole Foods and Trader Joe's the way country folk do when provided with actual shopping choices (I decided to delay agonizing over whether organic chain stores counted in my box-store boycott). Since I had moved to rural New Mexico, I had already forgotten how to drive in traffic. I had forgotten about freeways. I was the gomer people honked at and invited to join the twenty-first century with colorful hand gestures. Sweating profusely from the stress and the Venusian Arizona heat, I felt like I was watching a movie of myself as I handed money to a woman in an SUV in exchange for the Chihuahua-sized infant goats. My first thought was, if they spoke, it would be Spanish. I wanted to feed them Taco Bell.

> To feed three billion new people, more food has to be produced in the next fifty years than was produced in the past ten thousand years.

Janice the goat dealer had been waiting for me in one of those faceless business centers that are sprawling across the Tucson desert. I spotted her rig and felt like Columbo. Or the guy Columbo was after. Who meets strangers in a parking lot to pick up livestock?

It all seemed so sensible when we worked out the details on Craigslist. But real-world consummation of Internet relationships is weird in the best of circumstances. As I drove up to my contact, I thought, "So *that's* the person I've been e-mailing for a month. I had her hair straighter and browner." I suddenly realized I had no idea if buying large animals over the Web was legal. I looked around for a guy eating a sandwich in an Oldsmobile or some other TV-triggered sign of a fuzz tail. Oh, sure, like that parked van was really a "janitorial service."

Forget about what any cop or bystander would have made of this scene, I wonder what *I* would have thought if I had witnessed it a month earlier. This fit nowhere in the world of my suburban upbringing. I was as out of place as a Travis Tritt single on a heavy metal station. But as no one had bolted out of the van yelling, "Freeze, fuck bag!" I warmed to my task.

Warmed is too weak a word. The little nubby-horned goats climbed from their pet carrier straight into my heart. One was

snow white and commenced eating my beard as soon as I lifted
her. There was nothing I could do. Fighting it all the way, I
burst forth in a three-second rendition of the annoying
"Awwww" song. Fortunately, her sister, the brown-speckled
loud one, sneezed in my ear when I picked her up. This helped
me remember that the kids' cuteness was merely a frill. Much
more important, these creatures would be the centerpiece of
my new life on the ranch. I relied pretty heavily on the first line
of Jim Corbett's book *Goatwalking*, which stated definitively
that *"Two milk goats can provide all the nutrients a human being
needs, with the exception of Vitamin C and a few common trace
elements."*

Before I left Tucson, Janice (a perfectly nice housewife from a
nearby ranch who even brought me lunch) showed me how to
bottle-feed the pure white gumdrop I had named Natalie because I think Natalie Merchant's voice sounds a little like a
goat. That little kid went after her milk with a force that made
me glad *I'll* never have to nurse. I cringed and massaged my
own chest just watching her. I thought she was going to inhale
the nipple. But that was just the start of the unpleasantness.
Next, Janice pinched an area behind Natalie's shoulder and
said that's where I should inject the various vaccinations and
medications with the syringes I was to order from the soon-to-
be largest recipient of my income: Caprine Supply. Syringes?
Inoculations? Personally, I had to look away when I gave blood.

"The first few weeks are the hardest and the most risky,"

Janice said. I didn't know if she meant for me or for the goats. "Here's my cell-phone number. Call me if you have any problems."

I already had a couple. Natalie, who was revealing herself to be a heartbreaker and who started nursing my finger forcefully when her bottle was empty, clearly wanted to sit up front with me, while the one I was calling Melissa (as in Etheridge), whose horizontal slit pupils looked mildly homicidal and who bore a resemblance to Martina Navratilova, was showing signs she didn't particularly want to come to New Mexico at all, judging by the maniacal bleating.

I had been reading almost nothing but goat literature for a month, much of it contradictory. As usual, books failed to prepare me for real life. The classic goat-care bible is David Mackenzie's 1957 tome *Goat Husbandry*, and thanks to the line, *"The nature of the goat is disciplined, co-operative and intelligent,"* I had started my career as a gentleman rancher naively thinking that raising dairy goats would be easy. I mean, I'd throw them some hay, breed them, and soon enough they'd be giving growth hormone–free milk, with enough left over for me to barter locally for things like hay, buffalo meat, and massages. How hard could it be?

Now, with five minutes under my belt as a goat owner, one of my kids was kicking me in the pelvis as I tried to get her into my car. Still, the amount of effort involved in ranching somehow wasn't sinking in. Instead, I stared optimistically at the

animals once we stuffed them in my Japanese hatchback.
These little fur balls were eventually going to give milk. Milk at
the Funky Butte Ranch meant no more "carbon miles"—the
fossil fuels snuck invisibly into the meals I had to buy. Yes,
seeing breathing goats in the same car that used to carry things
like Wal-Mart paper towel forests gave me an "I'm not on Long
Island anymore" sensation. Where I came from, a vet didn't
have to be trained to examine anything beyond a cat, a dog, and
the odd parakeet. The only time I had even *seen* goats as a kid in
New York was at a petting zoo. But I thought, Of course the
goats'll give me a little trouble at first. I'd be scared, too.
They'll be fine when we get home and they see the sweet corral
I've prepared for them.

Meanwhile, we had set Nat and Melissa on a tarp with a bit of
hay for road-trip munchies. They had already peed all over
both. Melissa was butting the windshield with her tiny horns,
and I wondered if the scene was being filmed for posterity by a
crew from *Cops*.

We made it home from Tucson with only $600 in car damage. I
was cool with that. I looked at it as more Cosmic assistance with
my attempts to use less gas. And now I had goats ensconced on
the Funky Butte Ranch. I was a rancher! Everything felt so real
and tangible, if smelly. In fact, life was great . . . for almost
three hours. That was when the coyotes started closing in.
Their yips were the wild canine way of tucking napkins into
their shirts and sharpening their forks and knives. They knew

within minutes that two helpless goat babies were in the canyon. For them, it was like Chinese delivery. They were thanking me.

I had returned home exhausted and wet at eight p.m. I immediately tucked the goats into their new corral and prepared to tuck myself in. As a lullaby I played them a brief Charlie Parker tune on my saxophone, which either soothed them or sunk them into a coma. (The goatlike Greek god Pan loved music. So I started calling my goats the Pan Sisters because I discovered right away that any kind of tune transfixed them.) By nine it was dumping rain and a bolt of lightning had taken out a full-grown cottonwood about twenty feet from the ranch house. This was a sturdy, seventy-year-old tree, sliced in half. By ten the rain had tapered off and the coyotes were too close for comfort.

And so I quickly came to terms with the reality that delicious, healthy, local cheese, yogurt, and chocolate goat ice cream were not just going to appear on my kitchen table. The misconception that it would do so lasted less than one evening. Not that I was pleased to realize that goats in fact required ceaseless vigilance. I was pissed. I sprang out of bed in my underwear to find Natalie and Melissa trembling at all the unacceptable howling sounds. Goats like routines, I had read.

I couldn't be sure that the corral was predator-proof. Mackenzie encouragingly and uselessly explained to me that *"Our goat houses must inevitably be . . . a compromise between that which is most comfortable and health-giving for the goat and that which is most convenient and economic from the point of view of human management.*" Nothing about hungry coyotes.

From the middle of the corral I scanned the horizon of my new spread with binoculars in the moonlight, trying to spot the wild dogs and scare them off, but evidently they had learned how to outsmart a neophyte goatherd like me. I felt like an Idaho survivalist fending off a tax collector. The coyotes' party was about a quarter mile away. It sounded like five hundred children being tickled.

There was no point denying it. I had to sleep outside with the goats to make sure the local predators passed by on their buffet line. I sighed. I was attached to the little Pans already, and I could not face coming outside for the morning feeding to find four ears and a pile of coyote scat. Sadie, destined to be a live-stock guard dog, was still too young to be more than an appe-tizer herself. So out came my shotgun. It was strange and weighty in my hands, which made me feel like Elmer Fudd.

This was not going to be the comfortable night's rest I had en-visioned when we'd first made it across the river. At least the night was clear, though I had already learned how fast fronts could move in around here. I laid out my sleeping bag below the eaves of the goats' already dung-sprinkled corral cabana down the hill from the ranch house. After popping shells in my weapon, I tried to let the coyote symphony waltz me to sleep. "Sleep" being a euphemism for "continually waking from restless dreams of finger amputation to find a goat nursing my hand."

And I liked it. I liked being relied upon. I liked being responsible for my life (in this case my future protein). In fact, it kind of shocked me how quickly I was becoming one of those progressive-yet-Libertarian cowboys who listen to a lot of Willie Nelson—sort of the pope of this modern Rugged Individualist lifestyle. I craved a mass-produced domestic beer. But in an iced glass.

I woke up sore and smelly in the goat corral early the next morning. And, I noticed, promoted to the position of herd leader. The kids wouldn't stop following me around (and they haven't stopped yet). I guess the first bottle I fed them convinced Natalie and Melissa that I was Dad, or at least in charge of when the corral gate would open and wonderful things like hay, grain, and milk would appear.

I looked around groggily and processed that I was bunking with goats and packing a firearm. If I had suggested this as a career goal to a Long Island guidance counselor, he would have called for the men in white coats. Might as well make the best of it. Still casting moon shadows at first light, I built the Pan Sisters a jungle gym out of regionally unnecessary studded snow tires, ladders, and mud. I had learned from a majority of the "expert" authors that goats like to climb and be as high as possible. Who doesn't?

When I finished construction, I meditated for twenty minutes, thinking that I was a long way from my first batch of goat
milk. Even though they're physically ready to kid at nine
months, I was determined to give the Pan Sisters a fifteen-
month childhood, to break the chain of teen motherhood and
all its associated social problems.

Added to their five-month gestation, that meant I was a year
and a half from any payback from the beasts. Somehow it was
worth it, just to be working toward home-grown dairy products. I came from a world where there wasn't even a country
station, let alone the John Prine cult I now find such an important part of any healthy subculture. No one raised his or her
own food on Long Island. Where my weekly shopping list once
contained items like,

Orange juice
Wasabi
Preroasted chicken
Ice cream

Now I found myself browsing stores owned by Bush apologists
for products like,

Hay
Shotgun shells
Live chickens
Ice cream

I couldn't wait to get that ice cream off the list. Please understand how important this was in my life. Ice cream is a Food Group for me, which is why I'd gotten a goat breed, the Nubian, known for its fatty milk. And thus the Pan Sisters were even more precious. Precious enough for me to forgo sleep or even living in a house. As though to accent that thought, the day's first thunderclap rumbled ominously from the north. I went inside and put Pope Willie on the iPod. I figured I might as well get into character.

FIVE

HOW A FORMER SUBURBANITE CAN WAKE UP AS A FULL-TIME GOAT VET

'm not a big crier, and never in my wildest dreams would I have thought I could sob over a goat. But just as the Pan Sisters and I had developed a routine, I tromped down to the corral for the morning feeding, and found Natalie's nose running like something was chasing it. The next day she came down with a vicious stomach distress. The goats had been in my care less than two weeks. So much for my big ice cream plans.

It wasn't just the hideous mess in the corral that was freaking me out; when an animal who has already effortlessly digested two of your hats stops eating overnight, you worry. And when it's an animal you bottle-feed and occasionally rock to sleep, you worry a lot. The fact is, Natalie was clearly near death, and it hit me hard. These kids were the focal point of life on the Funky Butte Ranch—not just because so much of my plans centered around them, but because I couldn't ignore their strong personalities. Like the popular kids in the high school hallways, they always had to be carrying on some kind of conversation. And breaking every ranching rule, I had gotten sucked into these conversations. I'd become attached to them.

But I knew I had to buck up and shift into treatment mode, and fast. I started, of course, with Mackenzie, who informed me, *"If disease arises in spite of the . . . efforts of the reader . . . then call in the veterinary surgeon or herbalist."* Obviously not a book written in places that get hopelessly flooded by monsoons. No one short of a paratrooper or Navy SEAL was getting to the Funky Butte Ranch. So I Googled the hell out of "goat diseases," and after surfing to some links featuring quacks asserting that goat milk was the cure for every intestinal disease in people, I found out that Nat had a form of often-fatal parasitic diarrhea called scour. It could kill within days.

I found the treatment (a powerful scarlet liquid originally intended for pigs whose label contained ominous warnings about overdosing), immediately placed a rush Web order with Caprine Supply, and tried to keep Natalie hydrated for the day or two until the medicine arrived. It was awful to watch her: her eyes were filmy slits. I recognized the sensation: she felt as though she had just drank the tap water in Guatemala City. All

I could do was try to get her to drink and then drink some more. Not even saxophone serenading helped.

I was continually welling up as I worked at comforting my kid. I had been getting used to life as a goatherd. In addition to feeding the little Pans milk formula and hay twice a day, I ministered to their routine health needs (the Funky Butte Ranch kitchen counter at any given moment was strewn with used syringes, cotton balls, and a massive eye dropper called a drencher, which I used to force nasty oral medicine down their gullets), and every couple of days Sadie and I "slept" in the corral fending off predators. The kids had almost doubled in size during their fortnight in my charge (which wasn't saying much) and were probably the most carefully monitored goats in the history of animal husbandry.

In fact, until that terrible morning when I found Nat almost too weak to stand, I worried I had become one of those crazy, overprotective animal owners. After all, ice cream was at stake here. The evidence was strong: I was camping in the corral and fretting over every goat sniffle, and I had even posted a "Beware of Goats" sign at the entrance of the property to scare potential kidnappers away.

In truth, Melissa, the imposing bodyguard of the two, could take on any attacker, human, canine, or feline. Even at the tender age of six weeks, she wielded her horns with a precision that could get her a job with the Three Musketeers. In her overall demeanor she reminded me of Judge Judy with PMS. Natalie, on the other hand, was the snowy princess, demure

and snuggly, whose smile reminded me of my favorite grandmother. She held her hooves out to me daintily when I
trimmed them, like she was at the manicurist. Her ears, like
Melissa's, were half the size of her body. Strangely, she was
dominant over her much tougher, doting sister.

And now she was on the verge of dying. I felt helpless as I waited
for Caprine Supply to deliver the antiscour medicine. It wasn't
just vets who were shut out of the Funky Butte Ranch. I was
socked in. Even in a friendly rural valley, thumbing a ride with
two horned animals would be a tricky endeavor, not that they
could ford the river. It had rained every day since the goats'
arrival—sometimes for an hour, sometimes for six. The rest of
the world was off-limits to me, unless I was willing to swim.

Even routine feedings required me to fetch a little hay at a
time from the giant bale I had stashed on the far side of the
river. This was a life-threatening act, given the flood levels. It
also meant a soggy, mile-long, barbed-wire-hopping hike
every other day.

> New Yorkers, possibly because they tend to walk rather
> than drive, emit only one third the carbon per capita of
> the average American.

To make things worse, I got a panicky call from Margaret,
the local UPS woman, the morning after Natalie got sick. I was
in the goat corral stroking her tiny head when my cell phone
started singing.

"You're up to four packages now," Margaret wailed. "And one of them says, 'Urgent: Goat Medicine.' I can't get anywhere *near* your place."

This was a woman who believed in her work, so I convinced her to overrule post-9/11 policy and just drop my swag off at Lacy's house across the river. But how would I get the medicine to the ranch? Luckily, I didn't have to worry long. Just a few minutes after Margaret agreed to drop the meds off, Lupy, a lithe conservation organization manager from Silver City, called me up for a date. We had met at a book reading I did some months earlier.

"I'd *love* to hang out," I said. "But could we do it here? And, um, on your way over, would you mind picking up a package for me at Lacy's house? It's really important."

To just about anyone else on the planet, requiring a twenty-three-mile scavenger hunt followed by traversing a Class Three river with an armload of boxes would be cause for cancellation of a date, and possibly the end of all contact. Not for Lupy. I knew I was safe making this request. In fact, she'd relish the challenge.

This tall, blond, eminently strong young woman ran extreme races through the Rockies and competed in triathlons. Sometimes she won mountain bike competitions on trails I'd be cautious about hiking. Fording the flooded Mimbres River was hardly a notable chore for her. It was a thrill. Her idea of a sexy way to start the morning was to take me on a twelve-mile run before work. Before breakfast. Preferably including an icy stream jump. This was foreplay for her. She was Wonder Woman without melanin.

"Sure" was all she said. "See you at seven?"

I love mountain girls.

Humming "I get by with a little help from my friends," I kissed the goats on their heads and promised I'd be back in a couple of hours. It was time to trek for their breakfast. Nat wasn't eating, but I hoped that would change, and Melissa was ravenous. I put on my river booties and started hiking to the drenched riverbank, which was, for better or worse, my ad hoc hay barn.

And this was why, two weeks into the scariest flood even old-timers could remember, I found myself waist deep in the main channel of the Mimbres River. The supposed-to-be-gentle waterway by this point looked something like a Grand Canyon flume. The state's depth gauge had washed away. Overall, this was the kind of morning that made me wonder why Noah needed forty days and forty nights to get the message to live a holy life. One attempt to get across an engorged river was enough to set me praying, aggressively.

In fact, I looked like one of your more raving penitents as I held two pillow-sized hunks of alfalfa hay above my head after the manner of an Iwo Jima marine hoisting Old Glory. My face was contorted into a look of goggle-eyed concentration. Crossing didn't get easier with experience, because the channels shifted with each new downpour. The riverbed was a boulder field, an obstacle course designed to trap toes and dislodge kneecaps. If I stumbled and dropped the hay, it would be gone before I regained my footing. My whole life was now a game of liquid Twister.

But the goats had to eat. It was as simple as that. I was almost getting used to the fact that this was the way I had to import anything I wanted from civilization, anything dry at least.

"Stay toward the right side of the channel!" my sixty-ish neighbor Will Ogden called from a comfortable rock on the far bank, sipping coffee and straightening his cowboy hat. He practically lived in that spot these days. The flood was his principal source of entertainment, allowing him to share thirty years of embellished flood stories with the rest of the local ranchers, and one organic rawhide newcomer.

I tried to listen to Will's backseat river-fording, but from my vantage point the right side of the channel featured the same gushing whitewater as the center and the left side. One of our fellow neighbors was an aspiring pilot, and I made a mental note to inquire into hay airdrops, but the attempt to multitask caused me to arc precariously forward and two seconds later my cell phone and credit cards were soaked in my shirt pocket. You just don't see these topics covered in Louis L'Amour novels. No taciturn cowboy turns to the bonneted damsel and says, "Hold off those Apache, ma'am, while I make sure I can still send a text message."

I was almost halfway across now, though, and, scouting ahead, I thought I would make it upright today. I was dedicated to this, because drowning would complicate my plans with Lupy. It was my first date in a pretty good while.

I just had to survive the entire walnut tree that I suddenly noticed was angling downstream toward me like a torpedo. I'd been through this before. I timed my jump perfectly, and saved the hay the way an hors d'oeuvres waiter maneuvers a tray palm-up through a tight crowd. I heard Will applauding on the far bank and knew I was getting etched into local lore.

It wasn't yet ten a.m. Because an encounter with Will Ogden meant at least two hours of venting at the county for failing to build us a bridge during the four hundred years that Westerners had been hanging out here, I knew I had to get an early start on the goat husbandry that had abruptly taken over my life.

Though they slowed me down, I loved the community coffee klatches that formed at the swollen riverbank during the Great Flood of Aught Six. They allowed me to bond in inundated misery with members of the twelve households who lived along El Otro Lado Road (which means "The Other Side," in more ways than one). These kinds of connections could otherwise take decades to form in an insular rural culture where folks tend to speak softly and mind their own business.

At any given time during the flood, one to six stranded Otro Ladoans could be found gathered along the wrong side of their overrun riverbank in a sort of group therapy session to rationalize their questionable real estate decisions by cursing the government.

"We should all organize and refuse to pay our property taxes until they provide us services," Will was saying as I sputtered onto the far bank with my damp hay. "I mean, how could an ambulance even get *in* here?"

That was a particular bone of contention in our stranded Otro Lado minds at the moment. The wife of the valley physician, Mrs. Crown, was sick and needed to get to town for oxygen treatments. And this was just one in a series of neighborhood affronts. Everyone was still talking about Jake's narrow escape from his Monster Truck. A tractor had sunk during the recovery efforts. The Silver City newspaper had even run a photo of the carnage. We were feeling kind of famous.

"I think we should draw up a petition, demanding representation if they want taxation," Will inveighed, stamping his foot on the shaky bank.

By Day 15 of the flood, this was a refrain. I set down my hay and tamped river water out of my ears.

"OK, Will," I said, just as I heard the thunder getting serious. "You've been here for almost thirty years. Is there something special about this year? Or is it always like this at monsoon season?"

"Oh, it's always like this," Will replied in a softer tone, studying his boots. "Everybody gets all worked up, people nearly die, and then the river goes down and everything returns to normal."

I decided not to argue the very choice of the word "normal" in a community whose members paid mortgages on properties they couldn't get to or from, who lately risked electrocution every time they stepped out of their doors. Just as Will finished speaking, I watched an indigo lightning scar nail the hillside transformer behind his shoulder, taking out the electricity grid for southwest New Mexico for a couple more hours. Of late we had been enjoying power with the relative frequency of Baghdad.

> In 2003, 380 Americans were electrocuted.

As the day's first downpour went through its calisthenics, I turned back to survey the Mimbres River backdrop. The sky was a nasty bruise blue, and a heron was perched on a nearby cottonwood limb. Everything smelled like prerain ozone. Desert dwellers tend to gape in awe at the color green the way, say, a Floridian reacts to snow. But we had this odd surplus of chlorophyll. I wasn't even marveling anymore that our valley looked more like a Photoshopped fantasy of Switzerland than the kind of place where John Wayne hunkered down while in the act of genocide.

"Whatdya think?" Will called to me. It was the same question he asked me every day.

"Yep," I announced, spitting out an imaginary hunk of chaw. "Still too high for a Subaru, I reckon." Silently I added, "I hope this isn't too much to ask of Lupy."

"How're things going with you and Celia?" I asked Will, as I gathered up the hay. "Got enough supplies?"

"Oh, yeah, only problem is getting the grandson out to the highway to meet the school bus. How 'bout you? How are you holdin' up out there?" He gestured over the nearest ridge toward the Funky Butte Ranch.

"One of my goats is dying," I said.

"That's hard. First sick animal. Good luck with that."

"You, too. I wonder if you couldn't catapult young Reggie over the river."

"Hadn't thought of that. Might work. He's hardy. Could land on your hay."

I sighed and caught the top half of my reflection in a bankside eddy. What the hell was I doing here, trying to raise goats and pretending I chewed tobacco? I felt like Billy Crystal parodying a cowboy lifestyle. All I saw in the water was a scared freak in a straw hat and wet flannel shirt flecked with alfalfa hay feed. I could barely keep two head of livestock alive for two weeks. One of them was in need of emergency medical treatment, and the other was prone to sharpening her horns on rocks prior to attacking me lovingly at full speed. It was like living with Cato.

The kindness of my neighbor saved me from delving too deep into self-pity. "How ya doing for fruit?" Will said.

I almost laughed. The Ogdens had pushed enough of their heirloom apples on me that I couldn't close my freezer. Some grandparents foist toys or money on the young ones. The Ogdens foist fruit. My carbohydrates were accounted for thanks to two sunset picking sessions in their orchard in the past week. Both times, a cricket symphony serenaded me as I stood on a ladder and plunked into a bucket the tastiest crunchy-sweet golden apples I'd ever sunk my teeth into. I ate one, picked two, ate one, picked two. It was an orgy of crunchy sweetness in the rain. This was a variety that had disappeared from store shelves when everything at every supermarket got the McSame.

"I think I'm keeping the doctor away for at least a year," I told Will. I was cheering up at the thought.

Whining wasn't going to solve anything, I realized. I was stranded and continually soaked, but it wasn't just raining on me. Everyone was in the same boat. And from people with equal or greater problems, all I was getting was support.

Sure, I had to schlep a lot of hay and hitch rides into town for food. Yes, if Natalie wasn't better by tomorrow, she probably wasn't going to live. OK, I was no longer living with the comforts of suburban life. But giving up so soon would be an embarrassment. Even with my crack executive team of certified Realtors, three weeks would be pretty quick to flip a ranch.

Lupy showed up right on time, with Natalie's medicine in hand *and* with a carton of chocolate ice cream for me.

"Any problem crossing the river?" I asked.

"What river?" She flipped off her sandals and headed into the bathroom to change into dry clothes. A Thursday evening, I realized, as I dashed outside to play vet, could be spent far worse than in the company of a superheroine environmentalist who could leap flooded rivers in a single bound, out–bench press me, and stare down the meanest cow-defending rancher.

Natalie was too weak to put up any resistance to the drencher I pushed down her throat. Scarlet medicine dribbled over her lips like Kool-Aid, and she looked at me as if to say, "This better work." We'd know by morning.

Up at the house, I was so grateful to Lupy, I started to make her a Thai peanut stir-fry from the Funky Butte Ranch's first chard and leeks.

THAI PEANUT CHARD STIR-FRY

4 garlic cloves, minced

Handful of shiitake mushrooms

1 leek

¼ cup pine nuts

3 tablespoons olive oil

8 rainbow chard leaves

¼ cup snow pea pods

¼ cup carrots, sliced

2 tablespoons tamari

1 teaspoon Thai red curry paste

1 tablespoon peanut butter

1 lime

3 sprigs parsley

Over medium-high heat, sauté garlic, 'shrooms, leek, and pine nuts in olive oil until garlic begins to crisp.

Add chard, pea pods, and carrots. Top with tamari and red curry paste. Sauté, stirring periodically, until veggies are blazing hot but still firm. Remove from heat.

Stir in peanut butter. Squeeze lime over finished stir-fry. Garnish with parsley. Give thanks for the bounty and for all kind hearts.

I noticed as I was cooking that I wasn't exactly dressed for a night on the town. Bright red goat medicine stained my T-shirt and my coating of alfalfa hay was pretty much permanent. It was useless for me to try to "clean up" for a date or for anything else now that I raised goats.

In fact, I now emitted ambiguous green, leafy material on bank tellers and co-op employees every time I pulled a dollar from my pocket. It would have made me a little nervous had I lived in any state except anarchic New Mexico. Hay seeped into every cranny of my clothing, skin, laptop, and washing machine, to the point that I was constantly apologizing to supermarket check-out women and burrito waitresses. "It's, ah, just alfalfa."

"Too bad," their expressions said.

But Lupy didn't seem to mind: we stuffed ourselves on stir fry and beer and watched a Wim Wenders movie while the lightning danced outside.

I woke at dawn—even earlier than Lupy would have rousted me for a run—left her sleeping, and bolted to the corral. The world smelled of lemon because of these flood-loving limoncillo blossoms—tiny yellow powerhouses of olfactory joy. I wanted to roll in them, but I was on a mission, so I trotted on down the hill from the ranch house.

"*Mmbah!*" Natalie shouted in a strong soprano before I even reached the barn. I recognized the tone. It meant, "I'm hungry!"

I almost collapsed with relief. I uttered a quick but sincere prayer of thanks, since Melissa had joined the chorus, and soon the two of them would be waking ranchers in Montana with the racket. They didn't like it when I tried to do something unacceptable like write, sleep inside, weed the garden, trek for hay, or otherwise not hang out with them. They let me know this loudly.

"*Mmbah?*" one of them asked in an insistent, vibrato-filled bleat that I recognized as Melissa's hungry voice.

"OK! OK! I'm coming! Pizza delivery's on its way!"

"*Mmbah!*" Natalie growled again, which I took as, "Hurry up! I haven't eaten for two days." (This is a Gandhian hunger strike for a goat.)

"*Mmbah!*" I promised in a baritone, thankful that no neighbors lived in this part of the canyon. The goats and I often got trapped in this conversation along the lines of the "shampoo, rinse, repeat" loop. It was fun for me that they understood my accent. Even when they were out of the corral, one *"Mmbah"* out of me and they always came running.

A goat waiter in boxers and a cowboy hat, I was floating as the goats kept shouting. I had right-wing ranchers pushing apples on me, and pretty environmentalists fording rivers to save my goat's life. Love thy neighbor, indeed. It was the least I could do.

After the requisite morning exercise, Lupy made some breakfast (ice cream and leftover chard) while I went to meditate with the goats in the corral. Both Pan Sisters were back to their usual shenanigans. Natalie swiped my hat off my head as soon as I sat down, and Melissa hitched a ride in the wheelbarrow I had wheeled down to clean out the corral. Any goat book will tell you that both of these behaviors are clear indications of robust health.

Heather Thompson, my fourteen-year-old kerchiefed neighbor and the acknowledged Mimbres Valley goat expert, had told me it was never too early to start practicing the art of milking, so that the eventual nanny would be comfortable with the process after she gave birth.

"Do it every day," she told me. "You'll be thankful in a year."

You didn't ignore Heather when it came to anything caprine: if Martha Stewart did her own stunts, she'd look like Heather. She'd been milking since she was four, and was as relaxed around goats as I was around a Macintosh. So I had worked this into my meditation routine: sit in silence for

twenty minutes, stretch vigorously, then start faux milking.
I'd love to see this practice incorporated in a yoga book. In
fact, that's how Lupy found me to tell me breakfast was
ready: in lotus position, chanting "*om*," and massaging a
goat's nipple. It was too late to flee now. She had already
spent the night.

> The latex for safe birth control comes primarily from the
> tropical rubber tree (*Hevea brasiliensis*), with the best
> quality found in Malaysia and Thailand.

I left the corral door open so the Pan Sisters could have some
forage time of their own while Lupy and I breakfasted inside.
And how did they repay me for all my vigilance and doctoring?
As soon as I turned my back they beelined uphill two hundred
yards for my rosebushes—rose stems are goat filet mignon,
evidently.

The little bastards had forty-one acres of flood-provoked
wildflowers and bountiful, nutritious greenery to munch,
and when I discovered them, they were chewing my favorite
blossoms and stalks with exaggerated innocence. I could
swear they were smiling. I scooped up one kid in each arm,
tossed them back in the corral penalty box, and began my
fruitless yearlong attempt to build a rosebush Green Zone.
The fact is, goats can get into anything. Houdini learned from
them.

Over the course of the autumn, Melissa became the ringleader in this habitual assault. She was amazingly varied in her methods of access. And in fact, this clever, think-on-the-fly, intentional mischievousness is why goats are such incredible survivors. Where other livestock drop dead from thirst, they suck moisture from inedible-to-most Apache Plume plants. A flood comes? They can perch on the narrowest of high ground—say, a Subaru roof rack.

The problem was partly my fault: since I was herd leader, they wanted to be where I was. When I was inside the ranch house violating their social boundaries by eating a meal without them, they tried to get in with increasingly powerful horns applied to my sliding glass window. They actually knocked. And when that didn't work, like any kid who seeks negative as well as positive attention, they went for the roses. Especially once they had learned that was exactly what I didn't want them to do. Welcome to the caprine mind. They knew that entrée to the roses would bring me out running, screaming, and disciplining. But at least I was around.

About once a week they progressively decimated my roses. Sometimes it left me fuming and violating every parenting rule about not disciplining while angry. But no matter what the Pan Sisters pulled, I couldn't stay mad at them. They were so ridiculously soft and so important for my project that I hardly noticed that I, a boy sensibly raised on a modern diet of stuffed crust pizza and *Brady Bunch* reruns, was working on their well-being at the expense of nearly every other task in my life.

I didn't realize when I made a goat pickup off Craigslist that my "morning ranch chores" would generally take me well into the afternoon. That I could put "goat vet" on my tax return. That two little cunning imps would become members of my family. All they had to do now was stay alive for another five hundred days, and I'd be the valley's premier local, organic, high-end ice cream producer.

PART THREE

CONVERTED

*The use of vegetable oils for engine fuels
may seem insignificant today, but such
oils may become in the course of time as
important as petroleum and the coal tar
products of the present time.*

—RUDOLPH DIESEL, died 1913

SIX

THE

CARBON-NEUTRAL

PATRIOT

It was forty-three days before I could get the LOVEsubee across the Mimbres River. I couldn't help noticing that Noah only had to endure forty days in his highly publicized flood. But then he had to clean up after elephants as well as goats. On Day 44, as soon as I found my car keys (in the ignition) and started using fossil fuels again, I decided it was time to do something about the roughly 12,430 gallons of unleaded I'd churned in my twenty years as a driver.

One day during the flood, while I was yanking the Pan Sisters out of the roses, I'd gotten a callback from a mechanic I'd Googled up in Albuquerque. He proceeded to assure me that with a simple engine modification he could have me driving on the waste fryer grease from the local burrito shop. That sounded like too good an opportunity to pass up. But there was a catch: my fuel would be both free and carbon neutral, if (and this was a big if) I was willing to part with the LOVEsubee and get myself a diesel engine.

I carefully checked out this Kevin Forrest's website (his operation had the timely name Albuquerque Alternative Energies), and when it looked legit, I realized I half wished it hadn't. Parking brake lessons aside, I had a bit of separation anxiety when I thought about ditching a vehicle that had been reliably propelling me around North America for twelve years and 204,000 miles while spending about the same number of nights in the repair shop that Bill spent with Hillary.

But thanks to two healthy goats, I was on my way toward oil independence when it came to my dairy protein, so if I was serious about kicking unleaded once and for all, I had to take the next step. This meant crossing a few mountain ranges, and driving two hundred forty miles north to New Mexico's big city in what I hoped would be the final fossil-fueled road trip of my life.

I slipped and went down hard two steps into the Albuquerque Alternative Energies warehouse. My host, who pretty much lived in restaurant grease, didn't even notice. And so I got a second chance to learn that "stepping" is not the right way to think about moving across a concrete floor covered in vegetable oil. "Gliding" is more the technique. The floor was a nearly frictionless surface resonant of a glacier. Ice crampons would have helped. Regardless, my early tumble that March afternoon was a clue as to the important role that grease was going to play in my life from now on. Weaning myself from fossil fuels would be a slippery process.

"It's a pretty simple conversion," my tour guide, Kevin, explained as he led me inside the warehouse without so much as a "watch out—the floor's a little slick." (I had already figured that out and was dusting myself off in mild agony.) "It's just a matter of repositioning the fuel filter behind the lift pump, adding the heated VO filter, and bolting in a second fuel tank with a Hotfox unit in it to heat the fuel."

My eyes glazed over the way they do whenever an expert in any field speaks in jargon. Kevin, who bore the unmistakable aura of the mad scientist, had already convinced me he was going to make gas station fill-ups a part of my past. At the moment he was trying to describe how the system worked.

Kevin skated around the warehouse floor in coveralls that gave him something of an Oompa-loompa appearance (they were hiked up to wedgie levels), holding up engine parts for my edification. I tried to simultaneously train my attention on the mechanic and keep my balance on the warehouse rink. The twenty-seven-year-old didn't sit still for a second—it was like watching *Gilligan's Island* when they sped up the film to show that someone was really scared.

Maybe it's a sign that biofuels were coming of age, but Kevin
was so busy I couldn't figure out when he slept. Pounding Royal
Crown Cola from a three-liter bottle, he dashed between Kirt-
land Air Force Base, where he was an active duty Air Force Spe-
cialist, occasional visits to his wife and infant son at their
Albuquerque home, and the downtown space that Albuquerque Alternative Energies leased from, ironically enough, the
neighboring Chevron dealer.

For a pioneer in alternative energy, though, Kevin Forrest
was no tree-hugger. The two-tour Iraq vet sported a buzz cut
and made clear right away that he was firmly in the No Forgive-
ness for Jane Fonda demographic. I knew this because I always
like to ask military folks why they tend to support a coke-head
draft dodger for commander in chief (Bush) over a challenger
who at least *showed up* for military duty. Kevin said he felt be-
trayed by John Kerry's antiwar stance after his service. (The
future senator appeared at demonstrations with Fonda. Before
Kevin was born, but nonetheless.) So why was a fellow who
leaned a little to the right of Bill O'Reilly helping his country
reduce its dependence on foreign oil?

"I'm a patriot," was how the vegetable oil mechanic put it in
the warehouse, gesturing toward the Persian Gulf. "One day
when I was landing over there, it occurred to me that the people firing at me are financed by the oil that we buy and put into
our vehicles. It's a ridiculous loop. I just thought we should see
if we could put something else in."

We can. It's not even that big of a deal. Rudolph Diesel, the fellow who invented the engine that bears his name, actually intended for farmers to grow their own fuel. This is not processed biodiesel. This is straight veggie oil. These days it usually comes from waste oil from restaurants. No chemistry necessary. Just some filtering of french fry and sparerib bits. Stuff that would otherwise get sent off to commercial cattle and hog feedlots. Hence the fact that the Albuquerque Alternative Energies warehouse smelled like something between the local McDonald's and some Chinese takeout past its prime.

In fact, inhaling the warehouse scent while listening to Kevin talk about his vegetable oil system (a "VegOil rig" to us green geeks), it occurred to me that a plate of really delicious Chinese take-out left out overnight was probably the best way for me to visualize how the whole magical conversion of my vehicle would work. Imagine: I come into the kitchen in the morning, three quarters asleep, to the sight of my coagulated Kung Pao chicken leftovers. The sight always makes me want to retch. How did I ever eat something so full of chunky white fat globules? I wonder. And where were those fat globules last night?

The answer is: when my Kung Pao chicken was piping hot, they were tiny liquefied molecules about the size of BB pellets, pellets that flowed right into me invisibly. These small liquid fuel pellets were what I wanted going through my engine, Kevin said, though he put it in terms that only a senior NASA engineer would understand. What I definitely *didn't* want were those solid fat globules that form on my leftovers when things cool down. Kevin had developed a system of heat and fuel distribution that would ensure I was always getting hot, liquid Chinese food oil in the engine. Never goopy leftovers. And I mean this literally: my vehicle would run on the exact same grease used to cook the Kung Pao chicken I so love. And anything else that comes from the Heart Attack Accelerators known as deep fryers.

To make this experiment work, though, I'd have to get a diesel engine. Even under Kevin's veggie oil system, my vehicle would actually run on bad ol' traditional diesel fuel when I started the engine. But only for a few minutes. Once the engine heated up, the system would switch to a special fuel tank full of fryer oil. If this grease wasn't hot enough, though, it would clog my fuel lines like a Green Bay Packer fan's arteries. But once the system reached the magic temperature of one hundred forty degrees, I was carbon neutral: I could drive around the world without guilt if I wanted to.

SEVEN

THE RIDICULOUSLY OVERSIZED AMERICAN TRUCK

Buoyed by that encouraging prospect, I had started the day shopping for a LOVEsubee replacement. I knew I not only had to go diesel, but that I also needed a four-wheel-drive vehicle, because the last dirt mile leading to the Funky Butte Ranch was maintained with the frequency of the highway system in Somalia. So unless I planned on importing a smaller diesel truck from one of the wrong-side-steering-wheel countries, my truck would be (brr) from the Big Three and would come in one of two sizes: XXXL or XXXXL. I leaned toward XXXL. It's hard to convey what a leap this was for a guy used to driving a Japanese compact car whose only maintenance, for twelve years, was the occasional radio station change. But when it came to carbon output, I had an almost Swiss-like dedication to neutrality. So I braved what I knew would be a difficult morning.

> Toyota's 2005 profits were $2.5 billion in North America.

Just four miles from the Albuquerque Alternative Energies workshop, the Used Truck Sales Department at ("It's a Great Day at") Rich Ford in Albuquerque, New Mexico, in 2007 is a quaint throwback to every cliché about used car sales, right down to the good cop/bad cop sales approach. They in fact had a diesel truck on the lot, in forest green, appropriately enough. At one point in the negotiations I heard (or was intended to hear) the manager, from behind the half-open "private" door, yelling at my salesman that he would never budge on the price for such a "cherry" six-year-old vehicle as the one I was considering.

Frankly, I'm impressed that I left that day unsure if I was snow-jobbed or not. I was the one with the English literature degree. They were the ones with my money. Quite a bit over Blue Book. The whole thing felt suspiciously like dealing with used car salesmen. And when I asked the warranty department folks what pumping vegetable oil into my tank would do to any extended warranty I might purchase on my three-quarter-ton F-250 pickup, the response was unambiguous: such a move would invalidate it. That is the Ford Motor Company's official policy in the era of Peak Oil: you might as well dump sugar in the tank. How cutting edge. It made me wonder how this corporation could be losing money.

But I surprised myself by immediately taking to the Monster Truck I had purchased, the way a recruit handed a bazooka might become entranced by blowing up entire houses during target practice. I had with one large check transformed myself from the lowest vehicle on the road to the highest. I'd never owned a car with an entrance ladder before.

On my test drive I noticed tiny Hummers and Suburbans bowing deferentially out of my lane, their drivers smiling submissively and waving me on. I started reading clearance signs because of close calls at my initial overpasses, and when I pulled over I figured out quickly that whatever else it meant to be a full-size truck owner, I was now a parking lot refugee. I've since had scientist friends do the calculations, and it is physically impossible, in the Earth's atmosphere, to steer a 2001 Ford F-250 into a standard parking space on the first try. I suddenly felt deep empathy with every excluded minority. Before the morning was out, I discovered that all of us Monster Truck drivers congregate grumpily on the outskirts of supermarket and hardware store parking lots, taking up one and a third spots and suiting up for the long trek inside. Usually we leave our engines running, since starting a diesel V-8 engine (on any fuel) is such an event that three or more simultaneous starts can affect oil prices worldwide. Sometimes we hold barbecues out there.

A hybrid vehicle (like a Toyota Prius) uses about half the energy, and produces about half the greenhouse emissions of a full-size truck or large SUV (like a Hummer).

In short, it was an impressive piece of machinery. Before I had even declined the alarm system and undercarriage waxing from the Rich Ford Postsale Scam Department, I had named my new ride the ROAT: the Ridiculously Oversized American Truck. I mean, this was a V-8, which was twice as many Vs as I was used to. Suddenly I could accelerate up hills. Even when carrying four bales of alfalfa hay, eight solar panels, and a peripatetic puppy. I almost felt obligated to put a pinch of chewing tobacco between my cheek and gum, just when the rest of the world was abandoning its SUVs exactly like a bad habit.

And I realized at the first traffic light during the elevated drive to the Albuquerque Alternative Energies warehouse that the type of masculinity I project had now and forever changed. I went to sleep as a sensitive progressive and woke up in the NASCAR demographic. Women with names like Darla were eyeing my rig like it was a human body part. They winked. Introduced themselves with tattooed waves. Once or twice tongues emerged. I tried to put this in Darwinian perspective: was there something about excessive heaps of steel and insanely powerful engines that implied good breeding prospects? The LOVEsubee, compared to this vehicle, had roughly the power and environmental footprint of a go-cart. I couldn't believe they allowed such toys on the road.

Back at Albuquerque Alternative Energies headquarters, the vegetable oil conversion took three days, most of which I spent misunderstanding jargon.

"You can double your postpurge run time if you're getting hard starts," Kevin said late on day one, and I lost focus immediately. I didn't realize what an important point he was making. He meant that I had to clear my fuel lines of vegetable oil whenever I stopped for more than twenty minutes, or they'd look like John Candy's aorta. And the next time I tried to start the ROAT, coronary arrest would be the prognosis. I was so lucky to have such a feature in my truck. (If only we could purge the fat globules from our arteries after each Chinese meal.)

I wasn't concerned about fading out during Kevin's technical talk, because my truck was among the first equipped with a nifty digital control panel Velcroed to the dash. It was called the VO Controller and was invented by a guy named Ray in his Michigan garage. Thanks to this device, Kevin said, my engine would know when it hit a hundred forty degrees, and would switch to vegetable oil power on its own. It would even "purge" the fuel lines automatically when I shut off the engine. I didn't have to think about these nuances. I could just drive and feel like a green global citizen. Believing that was my mistake. It would take a couple of cataclysmic mechanical failures before I figured out that I *did* have to think about purging, and which fuel I was on. Often.

Even though we worked closely together for days, it was hard to know what Kevin Forrest thought of me. He confessed to having mixed feelings about all the "hippies" who kept wandering in wanting to barter four crystals for a full conversion of their Volkswagen.

"You gotta embrace your market," I told him, hoping my cowboy hat at least partly disguised my politics. In the background, the radio was announcing that Brazil had just become energy independent, thanks to massive sugar-based ethanol harvests.

Kevin knew his market, all right. In fact, he was thinking three stages ahead. Just as he punched out my dashboard and made my fresh-off-the-lot truck look like a critically injured neurosurgery patient, he told me that he saw veggie oil power as a transitional phase until someone figures out how to separate hydrogen from a water molecule in a sustainable manner.

"There just isn't enough vegetable oil in the world to power, say, the first million conversions," his head said, poking out from somewhere in the hood.

> VegOil driving is technically not legal in forty-eight U.S. states because it's not an EPA-certified fuel. In Germany, people have been legally driving on VegOil for twenty years. In the Netherlands, trains are powered by VegOil. In France, it's illegal.

I wanted a closer look at what he was doing to my ROAT. Sliding around on one of those square skateboards that mechanics use to get under vehicles, I looked up at all the colorful wires that were hanging out from my truck and wondered, Will there be enough vegetable oil for me? For the first time in my life, I was rooting for less healthy American dietary trends, to keep the fryer oil supply plentiful. I envisioned personally cooking a lot of french fries if necessary.

I think Kevin noticed my concern, because when he sent me on something like my tenth auto-parts run on the final day of the conversion, he asked me to bring back "something greasy" for lunch. "Gotta support the industry."

Kevin Forrest practically *was* the industry. In New Mexico, at least. He had recently partnered with a local waste oil collection company and opened the first government-sanctioned vegetable oil filling station in the United States. They got approval by offering both the State of New Mexico Revenue Department and the U.S. Treasury the same fuel taxes charged at gas stations: 21 cents per gallon to Santa Fe, and 18.4 cents to Washington, D.C.

"The government likes when you offer it money," he taught me. In March 2007, Kevin was charging $2.00 per gallon for veggie oil—while diesel was hovering at around $3.08 in New Mexico. They already had customers seeking them out from all over North America.

As I drove the loyal LOVEsubee to pick up lunch, I appreciated the savings, since I'd be filling up my freshly installed eighty-gallon veggie oil tank at Kevin's station. After that, I hoped, my fuel would be free: I'd collect the waste oil myself, from unhealthy restaurants. So, in the spirit of contradiction that seemed to pervade all aspects of my green life these days, I brought back Panda Express takeout. In Styrofoam containers.

After sevety-two hours and a dozen trips to NAPA auto supply, Kevin declared my truck "converted." As he was waving a monkey wrench the size of a golf club over the vehicle, his proclamation actually had a somewhat spiritual ring to it, though I've seen formal religious conversions that took less time. In fact, since I'd just gotten splattered head to toe in vegetable oil from assisting in a minor hose-tightening mishap that Kevin called my "annointing," I felt as though I had just been through what any theological scholar would call a religious conversion: immersion, sequestering, sleep deprivation, confession (of opposition to Bush), a visionary moment (the oil anointing), and, finally, tithing.

Now it was time for the first carbon-neutral fill-up. We test drove the ROAT to the Albuquerque Alternative Energies Vegetable Oil Filling Station and Restroom Rental Business in what can only be called a sketchy warehouse district in west Albuquerque. The guy Kevin partnered with on the veggie station also ran a lucrative porta-potty business. He was obviously a fellow who'd figured out a way to make a living carting off everything people wanted to get rid of before *and* after they ate their meals.

On the drive over, we talked about the delicate issue of world crop acreage being used to power Western ROATs, instead of poor people's food. Tortilla prices in Mexico had recently doubled, the radio was telling us.

"Everything is about market demand and everything is global," Kevin said almost angrily. "If these technologies are not cost-effective, they won't take hold. If some people need to find other sources of food, because crop space is devoted to corn, switchgrass, or grapeseed for biofuels, well, they've got to listen to the free market."

> Half of U.S. agricultural land is devoted to livestock feed, mostly cattle, and 70 percent of U.S. grain goes to feed livestock. Worldwide, 7 percent of the planet's biomass is being utilized now, meaning, to some energy theorists, that the human food supply is not in danger from biofuels.

I was pleased to discover that the kind of mechanic who once spat tobacco juice and whistled at passing women now discussed renewable energy for fun. Despite his "free market at all costs" mind-set, Kevin recognized that unless something compels the less ethical corporations worldwide to stop killing the Earth, the future is in jeopardy because we have to live on said Earth. And yet he somehow believed that Fox News was telling him the truth.

I almost couldn't believe my eyes at the sea of plastic restrooms poking out of the desert landscape when Kevin unlocked the

VegOil Station gate and shooed away the local vagrants. I couldn't believe my nose either. The smell of the facility was virtually anesthetic in its strength. Even the cactus seemed to be wilting.

Kevin looked over at me as we pulled in. I had my forearm pressed to my nose.

"It's the filtered grease," he said after I parked alongside enough sanitation facilities for two Woodstocks. "We render the whole raw mess, separating the good oil from the lard and the water, and the reject pile starts to smell ripe in the warm weather. If you weren't driving it, this stuff would go to feed the chickens we ate from Panda Express."

The actual vegetable oil pump, tucked between seven hundred porta johns, looked like gas station pumps used to look when my dad was little: quaintly oval, with an old-school gauge and actual physical numbers that turned as you fueled. I asked Kevin if this would be like a normal fill-up.

"Yeah, except if you hold the fueling handle long enough— *ow!*—it might burn your hand. Feel."

I clasped the handle. "Yeah, *ow!* Hot," I agreed. I guessed correctly that the pump was kept at scalding temperatures to prevent artery clogging in its lines.

With my palm still sizzling, I reached for the nozzle again with my shirttail as a potholder. I wanted to put the first vegetable oil into my truck even if it cost me a hand. I mean, filling up with a clean fuel from a totally old-school pump. How cool was that? I felt like ordering a grape Nehi.

I unscrewed my gas cap and aimed the nozzle at my normal fuel tank.

"Whoa whoa *whoa*!" Kevin shouted, breaking me out of my reverie.

"What?"

"If you put the vegetable oil in your old diesel tank, this truck'll never drive again."

"Right."

Just what I needed: two fuels to think about. But a few minutes later, with eighty gallons of vegetable oil in the correct tank and a second-degree-burned hand, I did a little mileage calculation. If I got the same eighteen miles per gallon on Veg-Oil that I got on diesel, I wouldn't have to fill up for the next fifteen hundred miles. That would get me halfway across North America. I was good to go for months, and I wouldn't have to fill up with actual diesel, well, almost never. With diesel prices up twenty cents per gallon in the three days since I arrived in Albuquerque due to some kind of pipeline sabotage in Nigeria, I was already rubbing my palms together.

It'd be so simple: when I ran out of veggie oil, I'd simply get more at the Mimbres Café. That was one of two small eateries in my valley, known for its mastery of both traditional New Mexican dietary staples: fried corn products and fried flour products. I could still tool around in a car, that ultimate American symbol of freedom. My gas would be free and clean. Sure, I would have to calculate and pay my own fuel taxes on the honor system next April. But that was a lot better than that last $67 diesel fill-up I had just endured on the nearby tax-free Indian reservation. I was carbon neutral, and it felt right.

EIGHT

THE
KUNG PAO
SMOKESCREEN

Halfway home from Albuquerque, I decided to call someone. I thought it'd be fun to say, "Guess what I'm driving on right now?" But as I flipped open the phone at eighty-one miles an hour, I realized, with a smart in my belly, that there was no one in my life I felt close enough with to wake up with a pop quiz in the middle of the night. I paged through my auto dialer. Nada.

In the weeks since Lupy and I had realized we were better off as running friends, I'd spent time with a woman who had a tendency to talk about past lovers practically while still in flagrante with her current one, and a woman who disclosed "I don't really have a lot to say." This wasn't the most satisfying period of my romantic life.

Still, it was truly thrilling to be driving on a carbon-neutral fuel. Just like that. It was the first time that I concretely felt like I was making progress in my experiment. I mean, I was driving. A Monster Truck. On vegetable oil. Above me, the stars south of Socorro were, as always, the most piercingly clear in this sector of the galaxy, and I wasn't doing anything to smog them up. It's just one of those amazing phenomena that while theoretically possible, seems almost magical when it occurs, like a super-nova, or Stephen Colbert speaking at the White House.

The only downside I noticed was a powerful craving for Kung Pao chicken. Even though I'd just eaten, I found myself mysteriously drawn to Chinese takeout places at every exit. Kevin had warned me about this. Now and forever more, my truck was basically a munchies machine. The exhaust smelled like heaven.

It was a small price to pay: the ROAT handled beautifully on veggie oil. The ride was quieter than on diesel. And the fuel gauge didn't even budge for the whole two-hundred-forty-mile drive to the Funky Butte Ranch. I could get used to this.

The problems began a couple of days later when I tried starting the beast for a town run. True, it was a cold morning at 5,400 feet elevation—even Sadie in the passenger seat was shivering. But I have never experienced a motorized vehicle so fervently dedicated to not starting. After ten minutes of deafening engine coughing that activated the part of my brain responsible for thinking That can't be good, I started seeing red.

"Can you believe we actually *unloaded* that rig on that rawhide liberal?" I imagined the used-car boss was saying to his salesman over beers. "He's probably stranded in the desert somewhere."

But then I got a grip, took a deep breath, and tried to remember Kevin's instructions. Starting a diesel engine *does* involve more prestart rituals than a space shuttle launch. I ran through the checklist. Plenty of fuel. Clutch engaged. I even remembered to turn on the glow plugs prior to starting. So I did what any intelligent primate with a well-developed cerebral cortex would do in such a situation: I went back to cranking the starter for another fifteen minutes.

Surprisingly, this technique sort of worked. On the one hand, the ROAT's mighty engine did in fact turn over, but on the other, my truck was engulfed in a thick, white, Batmobile-like smoke-screen redolent of a certain Chinese dish. It was probably caused by incomplete veggie oil removal from my fuel lines.

I heard Sadie yelping as she bolted from the truck and took off for the Funky Butte. I leaped down the two and a half stories from my seat and ran for cover, too. I was certain that something was gonna blow as I emerged into a world so saturated with smoke I thought I was in my high school's teachers' lounge. Maybe I should have been listening more closely when Kevin was going on and on about "purging."

I thought my digital VO Controller would handle all that. It had a feature specifically called "autopurge." I was learning that driving on green fuel was going to be much more of a participatory experience than I had planned. In fact, my mechanical expertise at this point had been limited to tire changing. I was now a full-time engine diagnostician. That is, if I wanted to drive anywhere, say, to the Silver City co-op for broccoli. Suddenly I missed the LOVEsubee and its quaint Japanese reliability. I still hadn't sold it—it was jammed into the Forrests' garage in Albuquerque, surrounded by piles of two-stroke power equipment. Maybe I wasn't meant to drive on alternative fuels.

But eventually the smoke cleared. I could see a tornadolike pillar drifting off toward Mexico at a height of perhaps five hundred feet. Somewhere in Chihuahua, a village was about to get very, very hungry.

VALISA'S KUNG PAO CHICKEN WITH COLD SESAME NOODLES

CHICKEN

3 chicken breasts, cut into strips

1 tablespoon Chinese rice wine

Pinch salt

Pinch white pepper

3 teaspoons corn flour

3 teaspoons Chinese black vinegar

3 teaspoons sugar

1 teaspoon honey

1 tablespoon soy sauce

Sunflower oil

¼ cup cashew nuts

3 dried Szechwan chilies, snipped with scissors or, if you only want them for subtle flavor, leave them whole and discard once the chili oil is made

3 garlic cloves, crushed and diced

1 tablespoon ginger, julienned

1 carrot, sliced

1 bunch of spring onion, only the white part, sliced

1 bell pepper, sliced

Marinate the chicken in the rice wine, salt, pepper, and 1 teaspoon corn flour, and leave to chill in the fridge for 20 minutes.

Mix vinegar, sugar, 1 teaspoon corn flour, honey, and soy sauce (this is your sauce).

Heat up some oil in the wok. Toss the cashew nuts in and fry until light brown. Then remove quickly and leave to dry. Set this oil aside.

Heat up 1 tablespoon fresh oil in the wok. Add the chilies but remove after one minute. Set chilies aside.

Add the chicken to the chili oil and stir fry for about 3 minutes. Add garlic and ginger and toss around in the wok before adding the carrot, onion, and bell pepper. Stir in the sauce and fry for about 5 more minutes.

Add about a teaspoon of the cashew nut oil.

Add the cashew nuts and the chilies.

Noodles

1 package lo mein or udon noodles
4 garlic cloves
1 bunch of spring onion, only the green parts, sliced
Handful sesame seeds, toasted

Cook the noodles according to package directions. Once the noodles are soft, strain and quickly rinse in cold water.

Sauté garlic and onion lightly.

In a bowl, toss the noodles with the sesame seeds, and garlic and onion.

Chill. (Might be wise to prepare noodles before chicken.)

Serve the chicken with the sesame noodles. Save waste oil for use in Vegetable Oil–powered vehicle.

It took a good half hour to convince Sadie that it was safe to come within fifteen acres of the ROAT. During that time I figured correctly that the worst was over, so I rambled off to town. Although like a young superhero who doesn't yet understand how to control his new powers, I emitted probably a dozen Kung Pao smokescreens on that trip, several of them after new-clutch stalls in fairly busy intersections, transforming them into nightmarish though pleasant-smelling indications of Armageddon. Strangely, no one seemed to mind. It's interesting to witness people both angry and astonishingly hungry. They yell at you in the intersection, but then seem to forget about it mid-thought, and pull off into the nearby Golden Dragon Restaurant.

"Yo! You can't stop here!" a cop called to me as he passed during my third stall, waving away my exhaust with his hand before adding, "Hey, it smells like french fries around here."

"Kung Pao chicken," I corrected. This was getting a little vexing.

Things came to a head on the drive home from town that afternoon. Right in the middle of desert nowhere, I stalled again. It was my fault, in a sense. Ninety-six years after the Model T, the engineers at Ford couldn't figure out how to put first gear more than a millimeter from reverse. Because the engine was still hot when I restarted the ROAT, the Kung Pao smokescreen didn't erupt. But I panicked when I noticed that the VO Controller didn't seem to have me running on veggie oil. Its display read, "Diesel Manual." I sighed.

After staring stupidly at the VO Controller for a little while, I stepped on the parking brake and called my vegetable oil mechanic for some distance mechanical advice. I didn't want to be driving on fossil fuels. I wanted to be back safely at home watching *Curb Your Enthusiasm*.

"Press 'Override to VO,' " Kevin suggested. I thought I heard choppers in the background.

"Done," I said. "Now it says, 'VO Manual.' "

"Now breathe in," Kevin advised. "Does it smell like Chinese food?"

The problem was, just that afternoon, a new wave of some kind of noxious desert pollen had exploded in southwest New Mexico, causing my sinuses to expand to the size of small balloons.

"I'm not sure," I disclosed. "I can't really smell. I'm not hungry for Chinese."

"OK, then sniff the exhaust."

"Pardon me?"

"Hop on out and stick your nose in front of the tailpipe," Kevin instructed. "If it's diesel it'll burn your throat."

This was odd. No one had ever told me to huff truck exhaust before. Still, who doesn't listen to a mechanic engaged in war games? I put down the phone and did it.

"It doesn't burn my throat," I reported. "And now I have a mild urge for won ton soup."

"You're on veggie oil," Kevin diagnosed. "Gotta fly." He rang off.

When I hung up the phone I had a realization: the VO Controller wasn't the controller. I was. I learned to watch for oil temperature, and to switch manually from one fuel source to the other after short trips or whenever I stalled and threw the autopurge function into turmoil. I was beginning to understand what was happening inside the ROAT.

This truck, like my goats, required supervision. In fact, after my phone call with Kevin, I couldn't help reflecting on the following stats:

Length of time during which the LOVEsubee never failed to start: twelve years (and counting).
Length of time during which the ROAT never failed to start: one week.

More important, though, I was at peace with how a fellow can get used to whatever life throws at him. George Steinbrenner. Hiking with wet goat hay. Taking off shoes in the airport. Driving on finicky waste oil. After spending my first couple of weeks afraid to even breathe on the VO Controller, I soon found myself tapping in to change its purge settings (sometimes while driving) like I was a court stenographer. And I had gained control of my Kung Pao smokescreens: sometimes, I confess, I still intentionally emitted one if I felt someone was driving too close or was sporting a preachy bumper sticker. But I looked at this as a carbon-neutral public service.

NINE

DIABETES
FOR THE
EARTH

The morning after my cathartic call to Kevin, I sauntered into the Mimbres Café. I leaned on the counter,
tipped back my cowboy hat, and said to Leslie the
manager, "I'd like to do you a favor. I'm willing to take your
waste oil off your hands. For free. I reckon it's because I like
you guys, and your chocolate cream pie is so good."

Leslie picked up a coffeepot, started for a booth, and said
over her shoulder, "Get in line, son. Some guy drives up here
once a week and hauls away all our used oil."

Foiled! Was my up-valley neighbor Gershon one step ahead
of me? He was the only other person I knew of in southwest
New Mexico driving on straight veggie oil.

When I called him, Gershon confirmed that he had dibs on the Mimbres Café. "Maybe you can try some of the restaurants in town."

As nice as it was that two veggie-oil drivers in Mimbres probably indicated that the UN-fearing clique in our valley was being diluted by the Karl Rove—fearing bloc, I didn't exactly like where this was heading. I wanted my waste oil to come right from the valley, if possible. You know, to live locally. So I tried to appeal to Gershon's hippie nature. (He ran an organic vegetarian deli in town, and was experimenting with growing algae to provide his veggie oil.)

"Dude, let's set the tone for how to handle independence from Exxon/Mobil," I lobbied. "We can do better than 'I got here first.'" Not that my reaction would have differed from his if I'd gotten there first.

Gershon was on the same page. We agreed to stay in contact and share likely oily hot spots, while basically carving up the entire county into grease fiefdoms. When more people came on line, we'd figure out what to do then. It was a very good ol' boy way of handling the situation.

Still, our conversation wasn't going to fill my tank. I left a halfhearted message at the other valley eatery, Sisters Restaurant, which was less than a mile and a half from the Funky Butte Ranch. But its two curmudgeonly namesake sisters opened only on weekends and their menu struck me as a bit too healthy to provide much fryer grease.

The next place I tried was the new Chinese take-out joint in Silver City. The owner there was happy to have me haul away the waste oil that he was paying to have removed by guys with names like Rocco and Scarface. But when he led me to that most disgusting of all restaurant areas, the "back loading zone," he was shocked to see how diluted his monster grease trap was. "I think my people are dumping waste water in here." I think is what he said in Mandarin.

Kevin had warned me about this phenomenon as well. When it comes to running on vegetable oil, neatness counts. The barrel-sized filter I had bought made it easy for me to be my own gas station: all I had to do was dump the vegetable oil in, heat it, and let it settle. Then I could fill my tank. But restaurants needed to keep their waste oil in separate waste-oil vats. Preferably with no partially hydrogenated crap. No lard. And definitely no water.

Suddenly it seemed like grease supply might be an issue. I never imagined waste oil would be such a scarce commodity—not when you consider that the default ingredient in this Diabetes Capital of the World is essentially grease. Traditional New Mexican food is so delicious specifically because it is thirty-nine variations on fried corn. This is a cuisine so greasy that the primary protein source for generations has been *refried* beans. They're not just fried once.

From the moment I left the Chinese takeout, I steeled my belly and considered it my obligation to survey and test every Diabetes factory in southwest New Mexico, and regularly. On every town trip, I piled plates full of chile rellenos, deep-fried enchiladas (in green chile sauce), and sopapillas. I started to hear "Plate's hot, sweetie" in my sleep. I wanted to be both a knowledgeable and a loyal customer before I started asking the owner to take me out back for a tour of the waste-oil tank. My suddenly less-than-clear complexion could be seen all over Silver City.

> Two cheese and beef enchiladas contain 646 calories and 18 grams of "bad" fat (saturated and trans fat). That's without the refried beans. An average adult should eat a total of 2,000 calories per day with no more than 20 grams of bad fat (saturated and trans fat) and as little trans fat as possible.

And my skin was going to get worse before it got better. The way New Mexico small-town culture works, I'd have to eat at Mi Casita and El Paisano for several years, and possibly get engaged to one or two of the owner's nieces, before I could discuss the bizarre issue of poaching the Dumpster yard. On the bright side, with each town trip I was satisfying my USDA requirements in most of the major fat categories for an entire month.

Before I owned the ROAT for a month, I started to worry that I would be a slave to Albuquerque Alternative Energies' $2 per gallon grease. I was no longer rubbing my palms together at all my fuel-cost savings and snickering at how understated I'd be when explaining to my accountant about the $212 in fuel taxes we owed.

But just when I was starting to notice genuine health effects from this fruitless grease search (I had gained eight pounds since the conversion), I finally got the call from Sisters Restaurant. Right in my valley. I could practically smell their food from the Funky Butte Ranch. I knew Sadie could. Best Reuben sandwiches west of the Mississippi.

"We've got six gallons of prime grease for you," sister Rita said. Other calls soon followed. KFC corporate headquarters announced it was moving to nonhydrogenated oil the same week as Rita's summons came, and their Silver City manager said I could come haul as much of their fryer waste as I wanted.

It had been decades since I had visited KFC—I had no idea they offered apple turnovers these days. I pulled up in front of the Colonel's portrait and security camera, found the Dumpster and grease trap area, and before I had finished setting up the special pump Kevin had sold me, an employee wearing a do-rag approached, carrying an armload of garbage bags. I was wearing latex gloves and had driven a huge truck up to a staff-only area. I looked more like an esoteric pervert than a thief. I felt I had to take the initiative.

Before he could say anything, I blurted guiltily, "Christie said I could take your waste oil off your hands."

He looked at me as if I'd just said, "I have an imaginary friend named Snuffleupagus."

"What for?"

"I'm gonna drive on it."

He watched my pump suck the sickly ooze into a five-gallon container.

"Do you just pour it right in your tank?"

"I have sort of a laboratory back home, in my barn. It's pretty easy, though."

"And then all your gas is free? That fuckin' rules. Where do I get one?"

And so another green citizen was converted. But that was only the start. While I was filling up, no less than eight KFC employees gathered around, alone or in clusters, marveling at someone driving on vegetable oil. It was like a tent revival out there. I found myself giving a sermon about things like carbon neutrality and oil company profits. I couldn't help it—the audience was rapt. Two guys in aprons asked me to take their picture near the grease trap. And to think that a year earlier I hadn't even heard of a vegetable oil–powered car. Just fifteen years before that, I actually *ate* at KFC. If my recent exhaust fumes were any indication, I'd soon be drawn against my will to eat there again. Sure hope that universal health care coverage legislation moves forward.

Fuel wasn't going to be a problem. Not in the short-term. Patience. That's all it took. There was plenty of grease for everyone. I was starting to see why, in perhaps the mellowest culture in the North American Free Trade Agreement, diabetes might be an issue, but hypertension decidedly isn't. Now I just needed

to avoid luring too much wildlife to the Kung Pao factory for-
merly known as my barn.

And I also hoped that the county sheriff didn't show up for a
courtesy visit without calling first. I now had weird, smelly
substances cooking in my barn to go along with the two dozen
goat syringes in my kitchen, all covered in a constant layer of
green, leafy alfalfa. Taken together, it would be a lot to explain.

As smoothly as things were going, there *were* a few side
effects to my greasy life. Namely, I was almost always covered
in grease. As was my steering wheel, laptop, shower handle,
and checkbook. I slipped on the ground like Dick Van Dyke
when I tried to turn doorknobs. Only the steamiest of showers
helped, and even those only temporarily. But as my first winter
at the Funky Butte Ranch wound down, I hadn't popped into a
commercial gas station in months, and counting. I couldn't
even remember which side the old fuel tank was on. That was
all that mattered. Without thinking twice I was able to put the
LOVEsubee up for sale on Craigslist, only slightly sabotaging
the listing by pointing out that the "cherry" vehicle had more
than 200,000 miles on it. I didn't get any serious inquiries.

PART FOUR

SOLARIZED

The use of solar energy has not been opened up
because the oil industry does not own the sun.

—RALPH NADER

$9.28 billion
—Exxon/Mobil profits for first
quarter of 2007

TEN

WINDMILL

SURFING

My cell phone rang in my pocket on the late winter day I started to turn the ranch's power over to the sun, but I couldn't answer it, for the simple reason that if I unclenched my right arm from my windmill frame, I would fall and not get up. I was ensconced on a bowed plywood plank precariously erected on the steel windmill tower thirty feet above the Funky Butte Ranch's well. The plank was thin and it creaked.

From this tenuous "floor" I was trying to mount the ranch's first three solar panels in a windstorm so fierce it would have a name if it had formed over Florida. The panels were to power my new, fabulously expensive solar-powered well pump. The pump came from Denmark, where they don't employ slave labor, and where they don't retail at Wal-Mart. Poor people in Chad don't own this pump. The boutique device was already buried a hundred forty feet below the ground, in the Mimbres water table.

If everything worked, the sun would make my water flow up those hundred forty feet, and then down to the ranch house. I had to admit, this excited me. Once I had water in the house, I was going to turn on the hot water solar as well, and then the ranch's electricity. I felt my days on the coal- and gas-powered grid were numbered.

To enjoy my green water, though, I had to survive the morning, which at the moment seemed like a long shot. I was, in fact, losing my one-armed grip about midway up my windmill. With my other hand I was trying to bolt the panel frames into the windmill. Only the tips of my toes touched the plywood that was supposed to support me and my contractor. Oh, man, did I want to avoid expiring at an age that would only be considered old to the Mimbrenos.

As though from a great distance, I heard my cell phone go to voice mail. I hoped that the call was from Michelle, a valley teacher I was falling for faster than my likely pratfall would carry me to the ground. Aside from that pleasant thought, though, my overall situation at the moment was starting to make me miss the time when I could just turn on a water faucet or a light switch without guilt—before I realized that I wanted to eliminate utilities from my life. I was nostalgic for my innocent carbon ignorance. Those 1990s had been such a simple age. Slower paced.

No, no—I directed my mind away from this line of thought. Wow, look at this view! Boy, I could see a long way from here. My clothes weren't just blowing off the clothesline far below, I noticed. The clothespins themselves were snapping in half. I could see all three of the Funky Butte Ranch's buildings, squat like gingerbread houses, beyond the teetering clothesline. A loose metal roof sheet winked frantically atop the barn. Even the ROAT looked small. I shot a nervous *"Mmbah!"* to the goats underneath me (whoa, they and, in particular, their horns were getting big) before remembering the one piece of advice I'd always heard about scaling things like windmills and skyscrapers: don't look down.

It was too late. I felt my belly drop to the ground, smoosh to two dimensions like a flat basketball, and then return to my body with the snap of an elastic band. There had to be a better direction to focus my gaze.

So I looked up. This wasn't a good call, either. Given the wind gusts not generally seen outside of Oz, the clouds had taken on an almost hallucinogenic speed. Unnervingly, they made it seem as though the windmill itself were swaying, giving me a wild, vertiginous feeling of impending death—like a falling dream. I clasped the windmill frame with both arms and tried to get my bearings. Then I closed my eyes for a moment and could hear my goats calling back to me in a weird, wind-carried harmony. I hoped I wouldn't land on them if I fell. For my sake as well as theirs. Did I mention the growing horns?

For a moment I stepped outside my body. Except for my abject posture of terror, I imagined I looked like one of the guys in those old photographs of the New York skyline construction. My hat had long ago blown off and was now somewhere in Texas.

I sighed. I couldn't even admit my fear, which made it worse. This time zone had exactly one honest and competent well guy. He was four feet to my left at the moment. His name was Jimmy O' and his schedule was booked further in advance than the pope's. The real pope, not Willie Nelson. Jimmy had blessed me with his expensive presence after literally six months of lobbying. It had been like planning a bar mitzvah, right down to the catering. We couldn't reschedule just because the spring winds had chosen to move in this exact day. It could be months, even years before he'd come back. So instead of pleading for my life, I had to force myself to assist in the project. This meant saying things like, "Would you pass the three-eighth adjustable wrench, pardner?"

I thought my act was working, though I was not having fun. And this trapeze performance was just for the solar panel array to power the dang pump. I hadn't even *reached* the house yet.

I tried to convince myself that hanging from a windmill thirty feet above the ground in a primordial windstorm is a great way to get some perspective, not just on your property, but on your life. And I could see most of both—from the view and from the whole "flash before my eyes" movie I was watching inside my head. The wind nearly carried *me* away toward Texas twice as Jimmy O' and I tried to get the three one-hundred-twenty-five-watt solar panels attached to the windmill frame. The good news is that if we *did* manage to tighten the necessary bolts, the panels would likely stay in place for good: anything that could endure these gusts wasn't going anywhere, ever.

Forty-eight inches away, Jimmy O' was as relaxed as if we were inside playing cards. He was actually whistling. I couldn't tell if this was because he had spent his waking hours swinging from windmills for most of the past two decades, or because he had chained himself to the frame. Myself, I was "free climbing." I hadn't known that chains were part of the organic life uniform. In fact, this is one of the things I don't understand about natural selection in general: how any organisms survive their first critical Darwinian mistake.

Still, I was aware of how lucky I was to have at least some control over my water. The water supply for cities like Las Vegas and Phoenix is in serious jeopardy in the next twenty-five years as the reservoirs formed by the dams that supply them continue to dry up. Rivers like the Colorado often no longer even reach the ocean because of too many country clubs in Arizona. Basically, cities like Phoenix and Vegas are not sustainable at their current populations and shouldn't really exist.

Instead, they are among the fastest-growing areas of the United States.

My Mimbres Valley, with its autonomous water table and fertile valley, had been an oasis in the arid Southwest for thousands of years. And it still was, but only until "too many straws are drinking from the water table," in the words of one Realtor who was sinking a lot of those straws (also known as new wells in subdivisions). I didn't know how long my well would continue to pull water at current growth rates.

> Household use accounts for 1 percent of water use in the United States. Irrigation accounts for 39 percent. Worldwide, 1.1 billion people don't have access to clean water.

But for now, my new solar panels could function effortlessly once they were up. The system was, in fact, simplicity itself: the sun-fired silicon of the panels moves electrons that cause the pump to bring forth pristine Mimbres aquifer water at six gallons per minute. With just two hours of sunlight per day, the pump would fill the rusty, old five-hundred-gallon holding tank that was nestled twenty yards away, up amid the boulders near the Funky Butte. From there, the ranch's water would cascade carefree of gravity in underground pipes. It had a hundred and twenty feet to go to my house, shower, dish sink, and, if the winds ever calmed down enough for me to build it, to a super-efficient Israeli drip-irrigated planting area way down by the goat corral.

Jimmy O' and his son, T.J., had already pulled my energy-sapping old-school electric pump and replaced it with the solar one. We weren't using the preexisting seventy-year-old windmill for more than an unintentional high-dive platform because Jimmy O' told me that compared to solar power, ancient wind turbines were as high maintenance as a West L.A. girlfriend. I could believe it. The windmill blades creaked and moaned like a torture victim above us, and seemed at any time ready to fall, smashing the panels and decapitating me and the goats on the way down.

Speaking of down, I was truly amazed to find myself still alive and safely on terra firma half an hour later. I actually kissed the ground.

"Hey, the wind's stopped," T.J. noted pretty much the moment I hopped off the windmill frame. Of course the wind had stopped. It had made its point. I stretched, thinking, Man, if I survived that, nothing can hurt me. Just at that moment, Melissa ambushed me from a nearby rock platform, leaping twelve feet without a thought, like a buccaneer swinging aboard a ship. She landed on my right Achilles tendon, causing me to suffer my first significant fall of the day. And she was only trying to say hi. As I wriggled in agony against a barrel cactus, the goat lowered her nose to mine and then bit it softly. I noticed she had a rose petal tucked tastefully behind her left ear.

"It's working!" Jimmy O' called a few minutes later when he

had finished wiring the pump to the panels. I limped over and looked at the well control box he had attached to the windmill frame at ground level, and indeed, three green LED arrows were pointing encouragingly upward.

Jimmy and I hiked uphill the sixty feet through a forest of razor-sharp mesquite bushes and I climbed the ladder to the water tank's submarinelike hatch. I arced my body into the cavernous interior until only my feet emerged. Yep. Water was definitely cascading in from the entry pipe. But from the look and smell of the flaking walls of the tank, I wouldn't be lacking for metal in my diet. It was like an Alzheimer's factory in there.

"Would you drink out of this tank?" I asked Jimmy O' as I hopped down from the ladder.

He climbed up and took a look. His voice boomed out through the metal. "Um. Maybe . . . I might. Sure. Why not? Just rinse it out a couple of times before you start drinking from it."

While Jimmy O' SCUBA dove into my drinking water, another question had occurred to me. I waited until he climbed down, covered in rust. "So, Jimmy. Will I get enough water pressure in the house now that I'm on gravity and no longer using my old indoor pressure tank thingee?"

From his reaction, I judged that I had asked a decent question. Jimmy O' looked up at my tank and then down to the ranch house, calculating gravity in the Earth's atmosphere. "Sure, you'll be fine," he said at last, but there was wavering in his voice. "I mean, you might have to run around in the shower to be sure you're getting wet . . ."

Still reflecting on that eerie prognostication, I noticed a truly horrifying smell as Jimmy O' and I made our ripped-shirted way through thorns and goats back to the windmill. It was emanating from the spot near the well housing where T.J. was fusing two water pipes back together. He was doing this so water could flow toward my world again now that the new pump was buried. It was like the odor of something long dead mixed with something even longer dead. I didn't want to be rude, in case T.J. had been eating a lot of greasy food of late, too, but when I approached, I noticed that the pipes, T.J.'s hands, and much of the surrounding desert were dyed a bright purple.

"What's that purple stuff you're brushing on my drinking water pipes?" I asked nervously.

"Oh, it's just sort of a cleaner, kind of a solvent," T.J. said cheerfully. "It's called purple primer. Standard stuff."

I paused a beat to process the way that my supposedly green life was once again bringing me into the most intimate possible contact with the world's most toxic substances. This gave T.J. time to add, "Also it kind of makes a chemical reaction so the pipes bond together. Sort of opens the pores on the plastic."

My stomach turned. What was the point of growing Mimbreno beans if I would be watering them with nuclear waste?

"Is it . . . safe?" I ventured.

"Oh, yeah, we use it all the time. It's approved for potable use. See?" He proudly raised the label of the dripping canister. "Supposed to mess up your liver if you touch it, though."

"Oh." I gingerly picked up an empty can of the stuff. The label advised "washing vigorously for fifteen minutes" in case of skin contact.

Wait a second, I thought. It's OK to *drink* this stuff, but it melts my most resilient organ if it so much as *touches* my fingers? Something wasn't right here. T.J. might have read my expression, because he said, "Once it dries, you'll never have to deal with it again."

But I wasn't so sure. I had a lot of plumbing ahead of me now that solar power was bringing cold water to my house. If I was going to turn on my hot water solar, wouldn't something have to bond *those* pipes, too? I decided not to fixate on it. My water supply was now green, even if the equipment to make it so ensured that it cost about a dollar per sip.

ELEVEN

MODERN

SNAKE

CHARMIMG

Not only was I stressed about creating a personal toxic waste site, I had immediate troubles in the natural world as winter petered out. Jimmy O' had warned me to keep a close eye on the water tank, because I hadn't yet installed a "float valve," a sort of sensor, that would automatically shut down the pump when the tank was full. On a sunny day (otherwise known as every day at this time of year), the tank was going to overflow by mid-morning if I didn't shut the pump off manually. I could turn it back on at night before I went to sleep.

It was with the glow of the green citizen that I approached the mesquite barbs and the water tank under the shadow of the

Funky Butte on my first solar water afternoon. I'd had a busy morning manicuring goats and couldn't get to the tank sooner. But I was smiling as I left the house: my luscious, chlorine-free drinking water was coming to me without a single drop of oil.

The glow lasted until a rattlesnake the size of Chile blocked access to my water source. I noticed, at a distance of perhaps five feet, that the snake was actually shaped like the wine-producing nation, and was in as bad a mood as Chileans get whenever you bring up the subject of Argentina. When it detected my presence (about half a second before I became aware of its existence), the serpent reared up to a height of about twelve feet, rattled horribly, and showed me that it had not been suffering from any dental problems: its fangs were as nature made them—large, and hooked like scimitars. I don't know why the creature was upset with me: I had no interest in the pack rats it was no doubt dining on under my long unused water-holding tank. And I told it as much.

"What do you want from me?" I asked, backing painfully into a mesquite acupuncture session. "You can have the entire ranch rodent population if you want."

Then a thought hit me. It was probably my fault that the area was such a fine snake habitat at the moment. I was the one who had waited until the afternoon to check the tank, and the overflow had created a small pond around the whole area. I was up to my ankles in it at the moment. This was the only standing water for easily three miles in any direction. Of course all of New Mexico's wildlife would be drawn to it, and this satanic viper would have to be stupid not to answer the dinner bell. Life does not exist in the desert if it doesn't respond immediately to water. I had crafted a zoo. And I didn't want myself, my goats, my dog, or my cat to be part of feeding time.

In its current posture, the rattler looked like the kind of thing that is tattooed on the arm of people whose motorcycle handlebars are higher than their head. It was a caricature I would have dismissed as exaggerated if I had seen it in a film. As I backed away down the hill toward the windmill, inviting the snake to enjoy all it could eat, I thought how kind it was for God to have given this scariest of Earth's creatures a giveaway noise to betray its position. I would've thought silence would be an advantage for something that needs to get close enough to my ankle to bite it.

Terrified as I understandably was, I also felt a complaint rising: most folks, when they gripe about hassles with their solar power, speak of things like defective pumps, incompetent contractors, or insufficient panels to do the job. Me, I had actually pulled off the first part of my installation, and some sort of biblical demon had to immediately appear to throw a wrench into the proceedings.

The fact that I now had a snake farm was a problem that wasn't going away, as I needed to check the water tank twice daily for the month it would take me to get the float valve delivered and installed. If I couldn't even approach the area, my pond was only going to grow, and lure more snakes. I thought this over as I retreated to the house, trembling. When my heart rate returned to something close to normal, I called Lacy.

Since he was a lifelong New Mexican whose daughter owned several pet reptiles, I thought my neighbor would have some suggestions for how to deal with the situation other than massive gunfire. Unfortunately, because he was a lifelong New Mexican, I never knew when I'd catch Lacy in one of his congenital New Agey moods. He was firmly, mystically in one of those moods this March afternoon when I called with panic in my voice. When I apprised him of the situation, Lacy said that a reptile in one's path is an "interesting spiritual message rife with meaning in this spring season."

My heart sank. There is almost nothing more useless than a New Mexican in a metaphysical mood.

"What you need to do," he told me, "is ask yourself why the snake is coming into your life right now. Between you and your water no less. The elixir of life. What is it trying to tell you?"

I could hear Indian flute music in the background, and truth be told, I was looking more for practical advice than philosophy. Something about using a twenty-foot fishing net doused with chloroform.

"It's trying to tell me it's going to bite my fucking leg off if I try to turn off my pump," I said.

Lacy started saying something about a snake's forked tongue representing the dual paths we face at any moment when I chose the path of hanging up. I decided to do some Googling on rattlesnake removal before he started talking about which crystals were appropriate for this situation. Web surfing, though, proved even less helpful than Lacy's Whoo Whoo approach. I came up with a confounding Wiki-age barrage of conflicting advice as to whether to do anything at all.

One site consolingly advised me not to worry about capturing and relocating a rattler because "they are sluggish, compliant, and slow to strike. Just use a stick and secure the snake in a garbage can." Another blog informed me that rattlers are among the fastest, most aggressive snakes, and the best course of action is moving to another county.

I decided to err on the side of the more dangerous interpretation. The next morning I went to check on the tank's water level wearing a protective outfit that consisted of padded chain-sawing chaps, a bike helmet, thick winter boots, and a machete. On my doorstep I drew the four-dollar Wal-Mart weapon with a satisfying *whang*, and feeling at the same time overheated, ridiculous, and like a latter-day samurai, I made my stand at the windmill.

Gathering up twenty fist-sized rocks, I proceeded to lob a preemptive barrage of artillery at the aged metal-tank area as I slowly climbed the hill, weapon drawn. I don't think I scared any reptiles, but I did make some profound dents in my water storage source.

The funny thing is, I never saw the giant snake again—but

this didn't reduce my fear level. The main effect of knowing that there was at least one oversized, pissed-off rattlesnake on my property was that for weeks every noise, from a distant breeze singing in the cottonwoods to a friend zipping a jacket behind me, sounded like a rattler approaching. I wore the suit of armor daily, and nearly decapitated several bushes.

The rattlesnake's rattle can be heard from a distance of up to sixty feet. Rattlesnakes are deaf.

This is pretty strong evidence of hysteria on my part—there is no mistaking a snake rattle for anything else in nature. Outside of a Bush press conference, it might be the planet's most terrifying experience to see the rattlesnake's hate and hear the noisemaker to accent it. But irrational though my reaction might have been—I nearly scared off the FedEx guy when he arrived to find some kind of maniac in chaps and armed with a machete greeting him to sign for a package containing a drip irrigation system—there is something about the unflinching totality of reptile emotion that makes me not so interested in learning to negotiate its nuances (if there are any). Mammals, I can understand—even a mountain lion has some kind of thought process. But when it comes to poisonous snakes, I'd rather they just go away. I could only assume that the snake I named "Chile" had moved on permanently. But I kept an eye out for it until well after my new float valve allowed my swimming pond to dry up. For several months my machete was never more than a few seconds away from me.

GRILLED RATTLESNAKE DIJON

⅛ teaspoon celery powder

⅛ teaspoon ground coriander

¼ teaspoon cayenne pepper

¼ teaspoon black pepper

1 teaspoon salt

½ cup onion, sliced

1 medium rattlesnake, cleaned and cut in 1-foot pieces

3 teaspoons Dijon mustard

Combine the dry spices, salt, and onion and mix well. Sprinkle meat with the spice mixture.

Once the meat is well coated, rub thoroughly with the mustard. Wrap and marinade for one hour.

Grill over a hot flame until cooked through (10 to 15 minutes). Remove samurai outfit and enjoy.

TWELVE

TOXIC

TURBULENCE

When it wasn't snake poison, it was purple poison that was on my mind. I guess my fantasy image of clean living contributed to my continued stress about T.J.'s violet hands. I somehow tend to manufacture reality so that what I most fear appears in my life. Maybe it's so I'll get over the fear. Whatever the reason, my haunting premonition about purple primer proved correct as I continued turning the Funky Butte Ranch to solar power. Within a week of the rattlesnake's appearance, the stuff was stinking up my life again. The chain of events leading to its return started a few hours after I frightened off the brave FedEx guy with my samurai routine.

As I waited the nine minutes for my impressively misnamed "on demand" electric water heater to prepare my shower— sometimes I'd switch on the hot-water faucet and go for a run, in anticipation of warming water when I returned—I got a call from Herbie. Herbie was not an ex-hippie. He was a current one, a gray ponytailed sixty-three-year-old whom everyone in Silver City described as a "character."

Herbie got his rep partly because he lived in a rammed earth home that was something out of the movie *Sleeper*, and partly because he had "retired" from copper mine work into full-time progressive rabble-rousing. City council members had been known to resign on the spot when they saw his name on the public comment list on water use and sprawl issues. Also, he looked like a human birch tree (6 feet 8 inches, 115 pounds). Behind his activism was Herbie's belief that the world is a place of love and opportunity rather than competition and greed. He wanted to help you as soon as he heard your story. And so his call that night was typical.

"So you're serious about solar-heated water?" he asked. He was referring to some wide-eyed hopes I had expressed during a lunch with him and his wife, Gail, a couple of weeks earlier.

"Serious as the revisionists are about sugar-coating the Bush years." It was time for the second stage of the Funky Butte Ranch's solarization. Herbie's timing couldn't have been better.

"Let's do this then. Here's what you need."

Herbie proceeded to rattle off a list of plumbing and mechanical parts so extensive and technical, I was very close to asleep when he finished.

"Doug?" he asked, after what I guess must have been a long silence. "You still with me?"

I snapped awake. "I didn't *start* with you, Herbie. I don't know what a three-quarter-inch threaded CPVC fitting is. I don't know what any of this stuff is."

"OK, meet me at Mr. Ed's customer disservice department tomorrow and we'll pick up your parts together."

That's just the kind of guy Herbie is. Not only was he helping me get the Funky Butte Ranch off coal and oil power, he had recalled an offhand comment I had made at our lunch about my efforts to avoid box stores.

"I'm using my new carbon-neutral vehicle," I had told Herbie and Gail. "To get to shops that sell me foreign stuff made and delivered with petroleum."

At this point I was doing everything I could to avoid hitting Wal-Mart and its preroasted chicken breaks. I was like an alcoholic, taking it one town trip at a time. But I still felt hypocritical. Just because a shop was local didn't mean it stocked local products (or, for that matter, excelled at small-town customer service). To add insult to shoddy manufacturing, Mr. Ed's, the Silver City hardware store, had a manager who made me feel like a criminal every time I tried to return, say, a broken Taiwanese screwdriver.

"Where's your receipt?" he asked. "Did you get this thing wet?"

I don't know what the Mimbrenos did for screwdrivers. But I felt compelled to stick with my plan to wean from Wal-Mart dependency. I guess I saw patronizing nonchain stores as a start—to sort of get in shopping shape for the time when there would be legitimate local choices in New Mexico. Plus at least at Mr. Ed's I was enriching a resident of my county (Ed), instead of shareholders of an Arkansas corporation.

Meanwhile, Herbie was proving to be my hot-water guardian angel. While we carpooled to Mr. Ed's in the ROAT, he explained how the sun was going to all but eliminate my electric bill. His scheme was to build this kind of homemade solar water heater, called a "breadbox collector," which he said we could erect outside my house in a day. He told me it would soak up so much heat that it would make my almost epically inefficient "on demand" water heater virtually unnecessary. That could bring my cost per sip of water all the way down to ninety cents.

"Sun's free, my man," he told me as we drove. "And there's plenty of it to go around."

"Yeah, but I've just put in a twelve-thousand-dollar order for more solar panels."

"Once the grid's out of your life, though, you'll start paying that back."

I did some math. "That's true. The system should pay for itself in seventy-three years."

It takes about $40,000 to $60,000 of solar equipment
to power an average American home by the sun.

"Did you figure in federal tax incentives?"
"Oh, right. Seventy-two years."

The status of solar tax rebates is always changing. For
the latest on state solar tax rebates anywhere in the
United States, go to http://www.dsireusa.org/. And for
the status of federal solar tax rebates, go to
http://www.energytaxincentives.org.

But then Herbie said something that changed my life. It was
something not fashionable to admit in civilized circles ten
years ago, when most survivalists lived in Idaho, plotting the
demise of people of my faith.

"That's one way of looking at cost," he said. "But if there
isn't a utility around to pay any more, on solar you've still got
yourself power."

I made a mental note at that moment, driving around Silver
City making the driver behind me unconsciously hungry for
Kentucky Fried Chicken: shop for enough spare parts to keep
this life going for fifty or a hundred years into any kind of un-
expected societal collapse. Extra panels, extra batteries, extra
truck parts, extra vegetable seeds, and lots of ammunition to
defend it all. And everything written by Borges, Douglas
Adams, and Jonathan Lethem.

Herbie laughed when he heard my resolve. "You should start dressing in khakis."

Herbie wasn't just certain that our water heating device would work (he'd been heating his own water with a breadbox collector for decades), he was making sure we'd have a good time building it. He opened the passenger-side window and took a loud, deep breath of desert air.

"This is how to spend a morning," he said as though we were picking strawberries in a meadow, while I vainly tried to park the ROAT in the outlying reaches of Mr. Ed's lot.

"Buying PVC piping?" I asked.

"Hanging with friends, converting a life to solar power."

In fact, while we shopped for Chinese-made but locally sold plumbing parts, somewhere in Mr. Ed's aisle where the sign read "You break it, you bought it—we are not responsible for your negligence," I watched Herbie seep nothing but total appreciation for everything that crossed his path. Whether it was a demeaning manager at Mr. Ed's, the uneven way I had trimmed my beard that morning, or the tea-pouring method of the waitress at the Chinese place where he diagrammed our breadbox project while I lobbied the owner for waste oil access out back, he treated each person like it was his first encounter with the species.

"Where'd you get that necklace?" he asked the counter woman at Mr. Ed's. "I've never seen that shade of green before." His words carried all the more effect because he delivered them in a sort of "psst buddy" street corner sotto voce.

It forced me into the same mind-set. And I wondered what it took to cultivate such a loving outlook day in and day out when there were rattlesnakes and hardware store managers on the prowl. I didn't wonder long. Whatever plague of optimism and good humor infected my hippie friend, it was contagious. By the time we picked up essentially a skyscraper's worth of plumbing parts, goat-proof glass, black spray paint, aluminum foil, and (despite my protests) purple primer, I caught myself smiling at everything, like I was a paroled prisoner on a sunny day. The secret was to find the light in everyone and focus on it.

After Mr. Ed's and the intentionally greasy lunch, Herbie had me drive the ROAT to J&S Plumbing Supply on the outskirts of Silver City. This place—who knew?—had a water boiler junkyard out back where contractors dumped old units when they bought new ones for clients. The owners were delighted to have us recycle two of the five-foot-long iron behemoths for some undisclosed purpose. They seemed used to Herbie's antics, I noticed, as we heaved the old water boilers into the bed of the ROAT. They didn't even care that Herbie's friend Frank had joined us with a video camera, and was filming the whole project for public access television.

Back at the Funky Butte Ranch that afternoon, it became clear that Herbie was right: the design for the solar breadbox really was amazingly simple. So much of a green life is, in principle.

All it involved was creating a big outdoor box that would cook water before sending it into the house. Its design would say to the sun, "send lots of heat here."

We stripped the sheet metal sheathing off the forty-gallon boilers (horribly bloodying our hands in the process), then painted their rusty, bomblike cores black for maximum solar absorption. Next we encased both boilers in a giant, glass-fronted "breadbox" we had hammered into shape, setting the whole thing in a place with plenty of solar feng shui (out of the way and facing south-ish). Then we decorated the interior with toxically produced aluminum foil wallpaper, to reflect even more sun into the black tanks. The fourteen-foot structure looked like what it was: a giant toaster.

All we had to do to finish the project was reroute the ranch house hot-water pipes to run through the connected tanks. It was as simple as that. Water would fill the tanks. The sun would do the rest. There was no doubt about that: inside the breadbox was like living under a magnifying glass—almost too hot to work in there at midday on the first day of spring as we spread aluminum foil. We even insulated the breadbox with the scary fiberglass stuff that had once lined the water boilers, so it'd keep the ranch's water hot in the mornings and in winter.

Renewable sources of energy—solar, wind, and geothermal—will supply nearly half of the world's energy needs by 2050.

This was the day I became a redneck—literally. It was that hot. This had been a long-term goal of mine anyway. A farmer's tan was far more appealing than a Chaco tan in local taverns. If my neck was red, my hands were redder. What with the sharp metal work, by midafternoon my tools looked like they'd been involved in a gory homicide, and my fingers, already gatorlike from living in the desert, now appeared as though I had just won a vicious street fight. My drill carries a sort of Virgin of Guadeloupe–shaped bloodstain to this day, which I will market as a miracle if I'm ever in a pinch. There's always money in miracles in New Mexico.

Injuries aside, we had a grand old time spilling half our platelets. Herbie was excited to be teaching me about the technology that had kept his power bills measly for decades, and his personal energy kept us motivated under the sapping sun.

"What drives a guy to spend his time building solar water heaters for friends?" I asked him.

"I accidentally bought some real estate in the historic district in Silver City decades ago. Now I'm old, and the government sends me one check and the stock market sends me another one. I don't need money, and I've got time on my hands."

"And blood," I observed.

"Hey, man, you are momentarily going to be showering and doing your dishes with water heated to a hundred fifteen degrees before it even *reaches* the house—that's most of the way to a really steamy shower. For free. So my advice is, don't sweat a couple of"—looking down at his own palms—"near-amputations."

Wiping off the gore on his shirt, Herbie rumpled my hair in a grandfatherly way. Then he said, "Another reason I'm here is I've got Stage Four prostate cancer. So I'm doing what I want to every day."

Herbie said this the way one might say, "Hey, would you hand me that bag of nails?"

In fact, that's what he did say. "I'm doing what I want to every day. Would you hand me that bag of nails?"

"Here ya go," I said, stunned. "So, I mean, how do you feel?"

"I feel great. I was supposed to go three months ago. I'm still here."

To say this all caught me off-guard is an understatement. Herbie read my face, and said, "I told you because I know you'll take it the right way. Let's stay on task."

He went on to assure me that by sunset, my electric water heater, which at the moment ran at a level equal to Bangladesh's annual energy output, would almost never have to kick on. I was getting greener by the minute. And learning lessons about how to live.

It was the putrid smell of purple that made me realize we had issues when we climbed into the ranch house attic to plumb the breadbox into my hot-water lines. I caught my first waft as soon as Herbie cracked a can. It was the smell of lifestyle contradiction. As soon as I realized what was ahead, I bolted back down the ladder to change into my Haz Mat suit, which was basically my antirattlesnake armor plus a surgeon's mask. Just like the Mimbrenos never wore. I was determined to keep purple primer off my person.

But there was no way. The way the can was designed, once you miraculously pried it open, it was impossible to keep from dousing your fingers. After Herbie passed me the can and I food-colored myself, I tried adding kitchen gloves to my ridiculous disguise, but the mighty solvent ate right through the latex—in fact fusing it to the open sheet metal cuts all over my hands.

I jumped up spasmodically the first time this happened, and Herbie looked over at me with patient amusement. I honestly didn't think this guy had ever suffered a moment of worry in his life—it's why he looked fifteen years younger than he was. For a fellow like me, it was like being a race car driver and hanging out with an Amish farmer: worry was in my life almost every day. If only from goat assaults on my latest rose bush defense.

To allay my fears, Herbie held up his purple palms, and said gently, "Ah, a little violet in your diet won't hurt you. I've been working with this stuff my whole life. It hasn't killed me yet. It was hamburgers, not purple primer that got my prostate."

"The primer eats the liver, is what I heard."

"Myth. You'll be fine."

No matter what T.J. and Herbie said, I still wasn't convinced that something so purple was harmless. They had to believe it. They swam in the stuff. And purple primer was just one toxic in my life.

In our petrochemical society, we swim in more toxics than any other culture in history. There were 1.4 million new cancer cases in the United States in 2006. I've always been freaked out by the *C* word, ever since my supermarket shopping days on Long Island. I'd hear my family discussing the latest carcinogen reported in the *New York Times*, and I'd seek out that Red Dye #6 or chicken skin in the supermarket aisle, marveling that poison could be sold unmarked over the counter.

What made it all the more scary was that new things were always revealing themselves as deadly. One day you think milk is good for you, the next the added growth hormones in it could kill you. (Whether vitamin D caused or cured cancer changed several times during my childhood.) That "benign" spray blanketing the neighborhood in a fruitless assault on gypsy moths? Actually, sorry, turns out it wasn't so benign. By my teenage years, I had no choice but to go through life with a constant, nervous "temporary exposure won't kill me" philosophy. Meanwhile, my grandmother survived two types of cancer, my mother one. I didn't want to have to keep the record going.

And this was why I was obsessing about purple primer. It was a symbol of every toxic substance I wanted out of my world.

By the time Herbie climbed down out of the attic a few minutes later to feed more water pipe up to me through a hole he had bashed in my wall, my nerves were frayed. My mask was slipping off my face, treating me to the primer's incomparable bouquet. Also I had an itch on my neck. If that weren't enough, it was easily 236 degrees inside my Haz Mat suit. I couldn't take care of any of it, on account of the organ-eating material on my hands. The truth is, I was scared. I really didn't want any carcinogens creeping into the Funky Butte Ranch. Hopefully the Big Macs of my childhood—about seven per week—weren't already planting a time bomb in my own prostate.

Meanwhile, the piping that Herbie was feeding me didn't quite reach the connector I needed to affix it to, and, pissed off, I guess I kind of yanked on Herbie's side. I wasn't really listening when, far below, I heard his muted voice shouting, "Hey, man, don't pull so hard—the cement on the joints hasn't had time to bond yet."

By this point, bloodied and increasingly purple, I was losing faith, but Herbie reminded me of the noble purpose of the project when I hopped down to help him patch the wall he had mauled.

"Hey, would you plug in the coal and gas for the drill?" he asked me, and I knew exactly what he was trying to say: that I was working to get petroleum out of my life by banishing the grid. If there was some noxious purple stuff clouding my pristine vision in these early stages, I could deal with that in the future. One step at a time.

And so it was with a light and appreciative heart that I went for a run with Sadie when my breadbox collector was finished and Herbie had left (after declining my offer of a swim at the new Rattlesnake Pond). I shut down the old seven-thousand watt electric heater, because I knew I was coming back to my first solar shower. Or I thought I knew. On my return to the house, as soon as I clicked off the iPod, I sensed something was terribly wrong.

I swore I could hear what sounded like a fountain coming from somewhere inside. It certainly wasn't raining outside. It hadn't for months. It was a pleasant enough sound, conveying a sunny day at Versailles. But I hadn't designed any fountain.

I checked to see if the kitchen or bathroom sink was on, but neither was. Then I thought maybe the noise was some odd, soft Laurie Anderson song coming out of my subwoofer. Nope. Well, it might not have been raining outside, but when I finally opened my bedroom door, I saw I was midway into a steady, early spring, eighty-gallon downpour on my new four-figure mattress. Water (granted, hot water) was streaming from the ceiling through the smoke detector and light fixture. Just as a sort of icing on the cake, I had stripped the bed to wash the sheets that morning.

Maybe I should have been paying more attention when Herbie had advised me not to yank the incompletely fused water pipe too hard during my purple primer freak-out. I smiled, and took it as a cosmic lesson to use non-fossil-fuel-produced, nontoxic piping and cement in future projects. I donned the Haz Mat suit and climbed into the attic to repurple my fingers. Then I dragged the mattress outside to dry, where the goats used it as a trampoline to gain rosebush access for several days. Me, I camped outside in my sleeping bag, watching for coyotes. Other than constantly sensing phantom rattlesnakes, it was kind of fun.

A Finnish company called Uponor (http://www. uponor-usa.com/) makes a piping material called Aquapex that "doesn't leach toxics into your water" according to New Mexico solar design engineer Tom Duffy (www.thesolar.biz).

I was so distracted by the cartoonish mishaps associated with my solar-hot-water effort that, by the next evening, when the pipes *had* dried, I had forgotten that the breadbox collector might actually *work*. I discovered this at the same time I learned what a restaurant lobster's last moments are like. The shower was at least a hundred eighty degrees the instant I stepped in. Herbie had drastically *underestimated* the power of the breadbox. Sure, as Jimmy O' had predicted, I had to take a few laps around the bathtub just to be absolutely sure the water was on, but when I did, it was so hot it was cold. I was scream- ing so loudly as I streaked outside, skin bubbling, that I found Natalie and Melissa cowering in a corner of the rosebushes.

At least catching the Pan Sisters once again massacring my

favorite golden roses allowed me to replace burn pain with blind anger.

"Hey, get out of there, you cud-breathed Houdinis!" I yelled, which had roughly the effect of urban votes on a Diebold machine.

These rosebush assaults were really getting to be too much. The smaller stalks of all four bushes were nearly stripped of leaves, and I didn't like what it all meant about who was actually in charge of the Funky Butte Ranch. On this evening, I noticed, Melissa's means of access was a mocking dispersal of the horseshoe-shaped "garden nails" I had used to fuse fake plastic chicken wire to the sandy soil around the ranch house. She had flung these aside with her teeth, one by one, and then limboed under the fencing. Natalie had, as usual, followed her sister in. I had to say, they sure could make thorny green stems sound delicious. They crunched them like they were Oreos.

Witnessing this, naked and burned, was one of the few times I recall wishing that I had searched under "meat goats" instead of "dairy goats" on Craigslist. At least then I'd get the last laugh. I didn't even get dressed from my shower. Still wet, I snatched one goat under each arm and frog marched them down to the corral for Time Out and weekly fence repair. Hollywood edits it out of the John Wayne and Clint Eastwood movies, but this is the life of the green rancher. At least Lupy wasn't around to witness this moment. I suspected it would come across as even more bizarre than goat-milking yoga moves.

After the solar breadbox installation, my fingers were vaguely purple for weeks, and my favorite pair of Carhartts still carried psychedelic plum paisley blotches following a dozen washes. But these served as fond memories of the project with Herbie, who was still going strong and terrifying local politicos, months after the breadbox was up and running. I saw him biking around town on the Fourth of July, and soon after that I got an e-mail he sent to a community mailing list in which he exposed a Silver City council plan to give local water to a developer in a sweetheart deal. It wouldn't surprise me at all if he beat back whatever was attacking his prostate.

With the heater up and running, my showers became instantly hot (saving a lot of water). They also became scalding to the point that they nearly removed my entire epidermal layer, leaving me looking like one of those medical models of the musculature system. Still, between the new well pump and the breadbox collector, my grid electricity bill went down 40 percent the following month, even before I threw up eight more panels on my roof, and turned the rest of the ranch's power over to the sun. At this rate, my solar equipment might pay for itself in only seventy years.

After going solar, the Funky Butte Ranch used 86 kilowatt hours of grid energy in June 2007. The average American household uses 888 kilowatt hours per month.

PART FIVE

GROWTH

It is not enough to fight for the land.
It is even more important to enjoy it.

—EDWARD ABBEY

THIRTEEN

SMILES, EVERYONE: AN ON-SITE INSPECTION OF THE FUNKY BUTTE RANCH

The Funky Butte Ranch was supposed to be a farm. That meant producing food, and the first surplus food that the ranch provided went to a bribe. Well, let's call it a political contribution. No, no, a friendly gift to a neighbor. One blazing afternoon, while I was cooking the usual batch of grease in the barn, with the usual syringes and green, leafy material spread all over the kitchen, I noticed a plume of dust rising from my black diamond half-mile "driveway." Someone had braved El Otro Lado Road. That was an event in itself.

Through my binoculars, it looked like, yes, it was an official government SUV. I had a brief moment of panic that all my innocent medicinal paraphernalia had spurred an investigation. But then I remembered that I had applied for rural status for the Funky Butte Ranch, which meant a drastic revaluation of the property's tax value. At least I hoped that's what this visit was about. I was relieved to see that there were no support helicopters overhead.

Two percent of Americans are farmers.

I had to prove to the county that I ran a working ranch. And I wanted to: I'd just heard on the radio that 80 percent of fossil fuel use is embedded in transportation and personal products like carbon miles in food. I was in good shape on the transportation end, with the VegOil ROAT. Food was next.

Plus, there was this pleasant fringe benefit: if the local government bought my story about trying to be a legitimate local food producer (which I was just starting to buy myself), it'd mean a savings of probably a thousand dollars per year over what the previous owner had been paying in taxes. And, it turned out as the approaching vehicle resolved into focus, the county assessor had actually come by personally to check out the situation. This is not Los Angeles County. This is not a place where investment bankers can write off "farms" as tax breaks. The assessor probably knew every property owner's name, especially those who voted.

I chuckled softly, like a maniac with a plan. His timing couldn't have been better. The goats were out of the corral, foraging just out of sight of the driveway, and the moment he and his staff appraiser stepped out of their rig and we shook hands, the four-legged animals of the Funky Butte Ranch sprang into action. The assessor didn't even have time to utter the words "So where are these goats you mentioned in your application?" before he was mobbed by two smelly, horned creatures as rural as rural gets. They jumped on him and nibbled his pressed pockets and I said with almost passive-aggressive indifference, "Here are the goats I mentioned in my application."

The assessor wiped something distasteful from his shoes on a rock, and we began our tour of the ranch. First I showed him my new monster array of solar panels on the roof—something out of the movie *Contact*. I kind of felt like I was on trial here, so I thought I should display some knowledge of the workings of the equipment.

"Solar power is really nuclear power, but the reactor is ninety-three million miles away," I said, pointing at the sun. "It charges these twelve golf-cart batteries, which in turn power my fridge and subwoofer. No Enron brown-outs here."

Americans throw out 179,000 tons of batteries every year.

"Even in winter?" he asked. His expression said, "So what's all the war about?"

"Oh, yeah, everything's on solar year-round, except for my

electric range. I'm thinking of replacing that with a methane stove—you harvest the gas right from your composting toilet. It's all the rage in India."

> Solar ovens (sunoven.com) can heat food up to four hundred degrees.

The assessor wasn't saying much, but something I said appeared to have made him feel slightly ill. He was also sweating a good deal, I noticed. He looked like he could use a beer, but I thought it would be unprofessional to offer him one. So I led the way across the Funky Butte Ranch to the barn, where my dozen new chickens were laying more eggs than I could eat. As we toured the heavily scented enclosure, the assessor made marks on his clipboard and then asked, "Are you going to use these goats and chickens in commerce?"

"Oh, for sure," I said, with what I hoped was casual confidence. "I already tip contractors with chicken eggs. Next year it'll be goat's milk, cheese, and double-chocolate ice cream. It'll be big for the local economy."

The assessor broke into a smile. I had uttered the magic E word. "I'm gonna approve your application," he said, pocketing his pen inside the chicken coop.

I blinked. The man had just saved me a grand a year, and this was just sinking in, when he added, "If you're ever in town—I'm sure a big fan of fresh eggs."

Now I eyed the official closely. He was dressed in an out-of-place button-down shirt and appeared to be using hair product. This being a county not known for its strict interpretation of most law books, I had no way of knowing if my assessor was just a scrambled-egg aficionado, or if he was trying to tell me something. Was he soliciting a campaign contribution?

To be safe, I said, "You bet. I always like to share the bounty."

And it was in the best "you scratch my back, I'll scratch yours" mind-set that a couple of weeks later I sauntered into the county offices with a carton of Funky Butte Ranch Grade AA Large under my arm and told the secretary, "I'm here to see the assessor on the matter of the eggs."

She wiped the alfalfa from her desk and waved me back. The assessor wasn't in, but I imagined myself overacting, nudging the carton into his appraiser's palm while looking in the other direction, the way that people used to slip twenties into their license and registration at traffic stops in Alabama. If it was my first ever bribe in North America (and I later found out that our assessor is actually known as a pretty honest fellow), at least it was an organic one. The Funky Butte Ranch was officially Rural. And I liked the idea of paying my property taxes partly in produce.

FOURTEEN

THE FUNKY BUTTE RANCH OPENS A CHICKEN BUFFET

I couldn't keep up with the chickens' production. Within a month of picking them up from Lacy's sister, whose flock was getting out of hand, I had five dozen local, organic eggs stuffing my fridge. (My new chickens themselves immediately got out of hand in the truck on the drive home when their box opened during a *Dukes of Hazzard* jump near my river crossing. The final-mile drive was like something out of a Hitchcock movie.) And this abundance came despite my eating ever more elaborate omelets, quiches, and frittatas three or four times a day. I was running out of cartons. And I could almost feel my arteries clogging.

These chickens were unstoppable: they were, in fact, the low maintenance delight of ranch life. On eight dollars a month of feed, they trooped around the Funky Butte Ranch in a jaunty line, pausing only to raise my cholesterol level with daily deposits in little nests in the barn. The actual egg laying was a pretty big event to the chickens, by the barn-rattling sound of things. Were they killing each other in there, or just ejecting eggs? There were always feathers all over the place when I went to gather the ova in the barn. The least I could do was fry them up. The chickens also ate all of my organic garbage, greatly reducing what I had to cart out to the landfill.

> Farmers in Virginia are testing poultry waste as a biofuel.

I hadn't even been sure that I *wanted* chickens, associating roosters in particular with violent pecking to the shin area. But Lacy's sister convinced me that I wouldn't regret it.

"And take one of my roosters—chickens are happier in a mixed gender environment," she said.

"Who isn't?" I agreed.

And so I brought Avian Flu one step closer to my life. Almost immediately I was providing my own protein. It was one more notch toward true local living. And it was nearly effortless. The rooster was chivalrous to his hens, and deferential to me (perhaps because he witnessed me manhandling goats out of the roses once a week).

Still, by May, I was starting to understand how the Chinese economy felt. I was experiencing uncontrolled growth. I dreaded the egg hunt awaiting me in the barn every morning because I was suffering an acute lack of storage capacity. If you are what you eat, I would have to peck my way out of bed in the morning. I didn't know what to do with them all. Distribute them to local delinquents in advance of next Halloween?

POTATO, PEPPER, AND ONION FRITTATA

1 potato, diced

2 teaspoons olive oil

1 onion, diced

½ red bell pepper, thinly sliced

5 eggs

1 handful fresh basil, thinly sliced

1 handful fresh parsley, chopped

½ cup Parmesan cheese, grated

3 shakes crushed hot red pepper

3 dashes salt

Over medium-low heat, sauté potato in olive oil in a skillet until golden brown, 5 to 7 minutes. Add onions and peppers, and sauté another 2 to 3 minutes.

In a bowl, beat the eggs, and add basil, parsley, cheese, hot pepper, and salt. Pour the egg mixture into the skillet with the sautéed potato.

With a fork or spatula, gently nudge the egg mixture from side to side, to ensure that it cooks evenly. Do this until the mixture starts to solidify and a crust begins to form around the edge, for 5 to 8 minutes.

Jiggle pan handle. When the eggs have set, remove the pan from the stovetop and place under broiler for 3 to 4 minutes, until the top begins to puff up and turn a golden brown.

Allow to cool, slice, and serve.

If shortness of breath ensues, schedule appointment with physician for cholesterol test. Or increase exercise regimen.

In the unlikely event of leftovers, the frittata can be refrigerated in an airtight container for up to a week—makes a great cold Italian-bread sandwich.

Lupy helped me solve the overabundance problem when we went on one of her prebreakfast half-marathons one lovely spring day. After we finished and sat down to a meal, I desperately pushed a dozen eggs on her, and she tried to offer me money.

"Yeah," I said, laughing. "Thanks for the sex and the friendship and all we've been through. That'll be $1.25 for the eggs."

"Hey, don't knock it—they're $3.89 at the co-op in town."

I nearly choked on my egg salad. "You're kidding. Really?"

And just like that I was a commercial farmer. Or would have been if not for the Patriot Act. In early June I found myself at the Silver City Co-op with two dozen eggs. I thought manager Katherine might want to sell them.

Katherine looked my cream-colored exports over, seemed to approve of them, and told me that before she could take them I first had to fill out some state security form to register as a food producer. On account of the world falling apart and everything. I didn't like the sound of that, so instead I started selling them to the new co-op we had in Mimbres—it was within walking distance of the Funky Butte Ranch and down the street from Sisters Restaurant. I could drop off eggs and pick up grease in one trip. Plus, the manager there didn't make me fill out any government paperwork and I didn't ask any questions.

I pocketed my first two dollars and wondered if I would have to declare myself a "Chicken Rancher" as well as "Goatherd," "Writer," and "Hopeless Internet Geek" on my next tax return. I envisioned profits in the tens of dollars. I was going to be some kind of organic Tyson tycoon. There was no end in sight.

It is crucial to the understanding of what happened next in my young ranching career to be aware that by late spring, Michelle and I were inseparable. Pretty on the inside and outside, the history and yoga teacher (Silver City really *is* crunchy) possessed all three of my dream woman qualities: a kind heart, a sense of humor, *and* plumbing skills. It had been love at first sight, and after a couple of months of hiking dates, suddenly half my dresser contained disproportionate numbers of halter tops and skirts. I finally had someone to call from lonely freeways in the middle of the night.

The problem was, the Funky Butte Ranch's animals loved her, too. On the days when Michelle needed to drag herself to town at the crack of dawn for work, she had to close the pet door in the ranch house, or else Sadie would follow her the entire twenty-three miles to town. This meant the disappointed hound would be locked inside for the hour or two until I woke up for the morning feeding routine, thus preventing her from performing her contractual obligations as ranch guard dog.

That's how the troubles began for my chickens. One morning in June, my day started with a nature documentary. One that made me forever alter my general pro-predator inclination and start rooting for the prey. Specifically, I was roused from vividly pleasant dreams by a piercing clucking scream. I'd describe it as a sound closest to the noise that will be made by the mother of the next woman to become engaged to Kevin Federline. Not the soundtrack with which you want to start your day.

I bolted, naked and groggy, out to the house's main room and was greeted by the sight of a terrified chicken tearing past the sliding glass window. It was my best egg producer: a Rhode Island Red I called the Great Red Layer. Before I could rub my bleary eyes in disbelief, a red-haired coyote, with open jaws, followed perhaps a foot behind her, and maybe a foot away from me on the other side of the glass.

It was a beautiful and terrible thing to watch from the front row—and quite a rush of a way to wake up, let me tell you. A primeval chase was on, perpetrated by an animal that doesn't have the option of shopping at a co-op. The Great Red Layer glanced over at me as if to call, "Security!"

As for the coyote, he was nothing like his cartoon icon—he was sleek, fast, healthy, and apparently without an anvil or Acme product of any kind. I watched in horror as the canine

deftly scooped the Great Red Layer in its teeth without breaking stride just outside the by-now almost military-grade fencing surrounding what remained of my roses. As far as I could
see, the predator wasn't even wearing a pair of Super-Jet
Roller Skates. There was no cliff nearby for him to fall off. No
oncoming truck to slow his progress.

As Sadie and I dashed outside shouting "Hey! Drop it!" in
our respective languages, the coyote in fact did the opposite,
and was gone into the butte's foothills before I realized I was
barefoot and my toes were pincushions.

Sadie was on patrol the next day. I had rousted myself when
Michelle took off and I did a little tap dance to distract the dog
until my girlfriend was gone so that we could keep the pet door
open and the ranch under surveillance. That day, no chickens
were attacked, though the survivors were freaked out and had
stopped laying.

We thought the coyote had moved on. To make absolutely
sure, Sadie made sleep impossible by announcing as loudly
and constantly as possible that the Funky Butte Chicken
Breakfast Buffet was closed, effective immediately. She took to
barking at suspicious movements in the air—the dog equivalent of shooting at anything that moved, and asking questions
later. She was clearly blaming herself for the casualty.

Myself, I was surprisingly upset, too. I knew I had to brace
myself for the cycle of life and death if I wanted to raise living
things in a healthy ecosystem. And in the parlance of the

rancher, "It was just a chicken." But it was the Great Red Layer. It was a Funky Butte Ranch chicken. My next couple of days were tinged with sadness.

Michelle's next work day was three days later, and given that we had spent very little of the previous night asleep (I recall we made tabouli and chocolate pudding at three a.m.), we reverted back to the closed pet door routine, so that I would not die of exhaustion. (Michelle, a compactly built energy bar of a woman with impossibly giant lake blue eyes, is one of those people who apparently doesn't need sleep, ever.)

As a result, at seven a.m. I was treated to an exact rerun of the nature documentary. This time I lost my rooster and the two chicks that my jet black hen Agatha had just hatched. Agatha survived with rumpled tail feathers, but when I found her cowering under a juniper, she was suffering from an understandable case of Post-Traumatic Stress Disorder. It wasn't a good day. Michelle came home that evening to an angry boyfriend sitting on the porch with a beer, a laptop, and a shotgun.

"Wanna watch *Hee-Haw*?" she asked, pushing the barrel of the gun in a safer direction.

"Dick's back," I said. "We're down to six chickens."

The coyote, who I had named Dick Cheney, had obviously cased the joint, observed the development of my relationship with Michelle, and studied our schedules and possibly even the intimate details of our courtship. He was living in an undisclosed location that was clearly within surveillance range of our bedroom. Using classic scientific observation technique, he had determined the exact two hours in the day (four days per week) when the chickens would be both out of their roosts and unguarded by Sadie. He was perfectly content to wait out the days when Michelle could sleep in. This, to my mind, is high-level thinking.

Once I realized what was going on, I began to see why a century of active, taxpayer-funded species-cide against these dogs has been less effective than a Fred Thompson campaign strategy. Coyote sightings are in fact increasing as people sprawl farther and farther into their territory. Though I was full of grief, disappointment, and disappearing protein, it was nonetheless hard for me to be unimpressed.

If the poultry assaults had stopped at this point, it would have been bad enough: daily ranch egg production had dropped from half a dozen to zero. My hens were emotional wrecks, and tended to stare at me resentfully at feeding time. I was starting to see the source of the barnyard phrases "brooding" and "chickenshit."

But the carnage wasn't over. Once it became clear to Dick Cheney that we were on to his scheme, he developed a new tactic: he waited until Sadie and I took our afternoon run. This damn wily canine was smarter than the combined mental efforts of two people and one Australian cattle dog. Sadie and I came back sweating and panting from an hour-long jog, a week or so after the last attack, and I couldn't help noticing that another two chickens were missing.

I don't know how he ate them so fast—all I came home to was a pile of feathers. They clearly don't teach coyote pups the same table manners people are taught. Much more swallowing than chewing was going on here. At no point was there time for negotiation, let alone shotgun diplomacy.

In another couple of days I was down to two petrified hens—Agatha and a gray lady named Gray Lady who had been lucky enough to be nesting in the barn when the carnage began. The two survivors, in a remarkable evolutionary leap, had figured out how to cower at all hours inside the barn, awaiting the end of this terrible chapter in their lives. My only consolation was that my early goat corral work had been good enough to keep Dick Cheney's dietary ambitions away from the Pan Sisters. Or maybe he was rightfully fearful of Melissa's horns.

The truth is, I couldn't blame the coyote. The only fair way to look at it, I thought, was to admit that if *I* shopped for fresh local chickens, why wouldn't Dick Cheney? He had almost zero carbon miles in his low-fat, high-protein diet. He was an environmentalist.

There were no more attacks on the chickens. There were no more brave chickens—only the two terrified hens hunkered down like Baghdad residents. So Dick Cheney switched strategies and went after my waste oil supply outside the barn. The container still carried a vague essence of Sisters' Reuben sandwiches. It was irresistible.

Unlike his vice-presidential namesake, the coyote clearly wasn't going away. To make sure the chickens, not the planet's most intelligent species, didn't provide more buffet, I had no choice but to secure the porous poultry coop with chicken wire so that the flock was only free range when I was around to personally supervise. A friend of Michelle's had another rooster to donate, and I headed to JD's Feed Store in Silver City for replacement chicks.

By this point, having survived a flood and repeated coyote assaults, the staff at the openly right-leaning JDs accepted me as a rancher, albeit that weird one who often tucked a wildflower into his cowboy hat. This fine June morning, I made my way to the feed-store counter, surrounded by people whose grandparents had fought Apache. I spent a half hour kicking back and discussing the advantages of one kind of sweet grain mix over another without, I hoped, being mistaken for Chevy Chase in *Three Amigos*. Then I got down to the point.

"I need a whole bunch of chickens," I said to Wendy, a braided employee in tight Wranglers. "At least eight."

"Eight out back!" Wendy called out, walking me to a cage the way an office-supply manager might show me where the printer toner was kept. "Got yourself a coyote do you?" She pronounced it Republican-style: *KIE-yote*.

"Smart bastard," I said.

"Smarter than some folks I know," she said. "We've sold a hundred chicks in the past week."

The deviousness of Dick Cheney had wide reach in 2007.

After feeding time that night, Pat from the new Mimbres co-op called and asked why my egg deliveries had dropped off so precipitously after such an encouraging start. I tearfully explained to her that I was living in an Animal Planet special, and the predators were winning. "It's been gory, and sad, and the only bright side is I can feel my cholesterol going down."

When I hung up, I realized that my reliable protein, if it was going to be homegrown, would have to come from the goats' milk when they gave birth next spring. At least until my young, second-generation flock started laying. As for the rest of my diet, agriculture would have to keep me away from Silver City's attractively priced Chilean produce section.

FIFTEEN

WORSE THAN
ELMER FUDD

'd already tried my other option for local food-gathering: hunting. Back in the fall, I thought that one deer would provide my protein for a year. I thought wrong. They say your blood type determines whether you come from agricultural or hunter-gatherer stock, but my choice had less to do with my genetics than my inexperience with firearms. In fact, a small but vicious scar bore witness to my near-fatal attempts at becoming a self-sufficient carnivore. I should've known I'd prove lower on the totem pole than the inept outdoorsmen of my childhood: guys like Dorf and Elmer Fudd.

Having never fired a rifle before, I thought I was being clever by doing some prep work before deer season opened.

After I had registered for the state hunting lottery, I started conspiring with local gun nuts, otherwise known as much of the male population of southern New Mexico.

My first outing that previous fall had been a gun training session with my friend Ant at the Grant County Shooting Range on a sunny afternoon in October. I'd messed around with a shotgun in Alaska, but I didn't even know how to load the kind of rifle necessary for bringing down a mule deer. Ant, in agreeing to loan me his 30.07 (whatever that meant), insisted on a safety session amid the Rush Limbaugh listeners at the range. I was all for it. I even bought the orange cap.

"It kicks like a mule," Ant warned, as we unpacked the weapon from its case.

Great. We can put probes on Mars but we can't develop a firearm that doesn't dislocate the shoulder? Ant shared this information after I ran to and from Wal-Mart to return (without being questioned) the incorrect-caliber bullets I had initially bought for the session. When it comes to guns and ammunition, New Mexico doesn't have a five-minute waiting period, let alone a five-day one. Children here who have never heard of Lexington and Concord can recite every word of the Second Amendment. When East Coast Democrats begin to grasp this, they might start getting some votes in the West. It's not about handguns and crime around here. It's about meat and antlers. And beer.

At the range, Sadie hid under the driver's seat while Ant and I popped off at paper cutouts of liberals, terrorists, and environmentalists. As I aimed, Ant adjusted my hands, shoulders, and feet until I was roughly in the shape of a bowline knot, and warned me about something called Scope Eye. This had to do with the bad things that happen to people who don't brace the rifle butt fully while keeping their face far enough from the magnified eyepiece through which they're aiming.

I learned that day primarily that firing a rifle is about a lot more than pulling a trigger. There were scopes to calibrate, official shooting positions to adjust, ear pieces to insert, backgrounds to check for safety, bullets to load into chambers, and prayers to utter. I counted fifty-four things to remember before each shot, more even than a diesel prestart ritual. With Ant there to stop me every time I nearly did something fatal, I wound up plugging a solid 30 percent of my targets that day. But it was all too much information to process, so I decided to have one more practice session back at the Funky Butte Ranch a week later, after the swelling in my shoulder went down.

I set up a small plant pot on the property line fence about a hundred fifty yards away, across the tangle of weeds I hoped would one day be my planting area. Then I tromped back up to my clothesline. I loaded the scary device. I aimed. I remembered about twenty-seven of Ant's safety tips.

Fifty percent ain't bad. But I was nervous. Something was nagging at me. Not a good feeling with a gun in your hands.

Still, I overcame a strong Darwinian hesitancy, contorted myself into a formal firing position called, appropriately enough, Modified Jackass, and pulled the trigger.

When I came to, I felt conflicting emotions. On the one hand, from the pain throbbing in my temple, forehead, and nose, I recognized that I was definitely alive. So that was a relief. Continued life is generally my goal. On the other hand, thick scarlet globules of blood were dripping at one-second intervals from above my right eye, and in fact, the whole right side of my face and head was a circle of pain. The first sensation, that of relief, won out. In fact, it was buoyed when I saw that I had hit my target—the plant pot was half gone. I staggered inside, where I stemmed and treated the wound—a classic case of Scope Eye—with aloe.

"Give up hunting," I said to the scary fellow staring horrified at me in the mirror. "Even NFL quarterbacks call it quits after four or five concussions." Between goat wrestling and general ranch maintenance, I'd suffered at least half a dozen head injuries and tetanus-risking punctures since implementing my simple rural life. But this one was by far the most serious. I carry the scar to this day.

I didn't give it up. The lesson painfully learned (Gun Thing to Remember #28: brace rifle against shoulder to blunt recoil), when deer season arrived, Sadie and I tramped around New Mexico for four pleasant days, not seeing anything larger than a rabbit. It wasn't until I returned home and nearly drove on

top of three legal bucks on the last stretch of road to the ranch—
any of which would have been perfectly fine for me to shoot before new rules restricted my legal hunting area—that I learned
from my friend Joey that (a) having a dog with me on my hunt
ensured no deer in its right mind would be within a mile of me
and (b) having a dog with me on my hunt was illegal.

Live and learn. On the bright side, I might have been the
only hunter in New Mexico history to have his laptop, complete
with wireless Internet, with him as he aimed for dinner, and so
I sent a lot of colorful e-mails to friends about sunsets and the
poetry of subsistence from my homemade deer blind. I had
packed local bean burritos for the trip, so Sadie and I ate quite
splendidly as well. As we dined, we listened to NPR.

Joey, hearing this pathetic tale, took pity on me, and twice
took me out hunting birds with him during the winter. He told
me he'd spent several years subsisting on quail, dove, and
desert hare. It seemed like a good way to start, though I had
some qualms about shooting the universal symbol for peace.
But I needn't have worried. The grand tally at the end of the two
daylong trips was:

Joey: 11 quail, 16 doves, 5 hare
Me: 1 worm-ridden hare

I'm not sure if this was a simple matter of marksmanship,
the fact that Joey had something like fifty-five years hunting
experience under his belt, or my ambivalence about blasting
innocent doves to kingdom come. Regardless, the lesson was

that I wasn't going to fill my larder via hunting. Not my first year. I was considering taking some bowhunting lessons, which seemed like a more sustainable method than gunpowder and lead anyway. But if my tribe had been the one to dominate at the dawn of our species, you could pretty much scratch the "hunter" part off hunter-gatherer. It was cultivate food, starve, or revert to preroasted rotisserie chicken.

SIXTEEN

CHICKEN LITTLE
WAS RIGHT
TO BE
WORRIED

You can't just throw seeds in the desert and expect to eat three months later. Even if something other than a cactus miraculously grows, you'll suddenly be so popular with the local wildlife that your best bet is to switch back to hunting. The New Mexican squirrels alone are so fond of their veggies that Dudley, the slightly conspiratorial farmer who sold me my organic apple saplings, told me I'd do well to consider the kind of varmint traps that featured pry-apart metal jaws. I had inherited a few of these in the Funky Butte Ranch barn. I was scared to go near them.

> Desertification and other land degradation could be responsible for 30 percent of greenhouse gas emissions.

Deflated, I asked, "Should I even bother planting crops at all?"

"Either that or give it up," he suggested.

"Go back to Dominoes and the supermarket, you mean."

"That's really your only other option."

"Maybe not for long."

"Nope."

And so, on to organic gentleman farming in the desert. Enclosing my planting area was my first task, just at the time of year when even sunspots start to think my valley is a little too hot. With the help of my friend Abbot I threw up fifteen hundred square feet of egg-shaped antivarmint fencing next to the goat corral. I chose the spot because it was flat and a water line from the well ran right to it.

Fence building is hard: you have to maintain fierce tension on the fencing or it droops in the middle like Bush's approval ratings. It took us five long days, compounded by the fact that Abbot was a Rainbow Family member, which meant marijuana was part of his religion. I think it's important to always try to honor another's faith. And he was strict about it. Orthodox, you might say.

But finally the fence looked done to me, if not as absolutely uniform as I had intended. It was five feet high, and sturdy enough to keep the goats out. I was satisfied for the day or two, until I learned that elk can jump eight feet as though stepping on a sidewalk. So I wove the top of the whole fence with perhaps one hundred strands of bamboo grown by my neighbor Mr. Pittman, in exchange for a share of the produce grown. This touch lent the whole area a vaguely *Apocalypse Now* feel. I envisioned calling the State Game and Fish Department to ask about the legality of eating an impaled elk.

Then I had to bury chicken wire a foot deep around the entire area because Dudley told me that the damn burrowing squirrels could get *under* my new fence. I realized, dehydrated and with my work just beginning, that I was going to have to produce quite a bounty of food to earn back the calories I was spending in advance of sinking a single seed.

The fence done, I still wasn't ready to plant. Because Saharan sand masquerading as "soil" is the number one problem with agriculture in the desert, I had to untangle, figure out, and assemble the Byzantine network of tubes, valves, and spigots that comprised my drip irrigation system. It all came coiled in a giant box that exploded out at me like a jack-in-the-box when I opened it.

> Every year, 62,000 square miles of land loses its vegetation.

Connecting the system's 1,542 parts (many of them microscopic) in my new planting area involved punching drip holes in hose, plotting crop spacing, and setting timers—essentially the exact set of design, construction, and agricultural skills I was born without. When I was a kid, I had trouble building with Legos. I was no Michael Pollan *or* Frank Lloyd Wright.

Still, once my irrigation labyrinth was set up, I'm sure I would've immediately started conserving thousands of gallons of water if it weren't for all the inadvertent "drips" the system initially emitted from my installation mistakes. I spent another couple of days plugging those.

Now it was time to fertilize. The Funky Butte Ranch suffered no shortage in that department. Goat ranches are nothing if not fertilizer factories. I began throwing the goat-milk-duds-and-hay from corral cleanings on the planting area. This wasn't so easy, given Melissa's proclivity for hitching wheelbarrow rides, but all my neighbors were telling me that this mixture was the ideal fertilizer-mulch. Rather than super-fertile soil, though, the resulting ground just started looking to me like dung-covered desert.

Still, seeds got planted, and to my almost ecstatic delight, even sprouted! Michelle and I danced around the planting area like wood elves on the morning we noticed the first pea pods had started creeping up their netting. In keeping with my local-living intentions, the garden was focusing on the Mimbreno triumvirate—exactly what my fabulously if temporarily successful forebears grew, possibly on this very spot: corn, beans, and squash. All Southwest varieties. Plus, I was giving some other produce I love a shot: local "Mimbres Giant" green chile peppers, and not-so-local eggplant, brussels sprouts, broccoli, chard, tomatoes, peas, leeks, carrots, cukes, zukes, lettuce, and beets. It was a big planting area. I figured I'd barter with any surplus.

Estimated population of my county in 1000 CE: 9,000.
Estimated population of my county today: 31,250.

The drip system worked like a charm, although it seemed mainly useful for the production of almost supernatural weeds. Euphoric with the surprise bonanza of water dripping on them for a couple of hours per day, and knowing that a pesky farmer might at any moment try to pull them, these unwanted plants tended to be sharper than Dennis Miller monologues. They grew two feet per day in amazing variety right where my local corn was supposed to dominate the soil. Crazy gourdlike things and tiny viscid wildflowers with roots that extended to China invaded like flowers from a magician's sleeve. Overnight, a thousand vines of an annoying plant called spiny amaranth lasciviously entangled my plastic drip lines. I pulled them, and there they were again, the next morning. It was like something out of *Little Shop of Horrors*.

"It's taking us an hour to weed one row of peppers," I had complained to Michelle one morning.

"We could let the goats in," she said.

I looked behind me. Indeed, the Pan Sisters were foraging away on the same amaranth right outside the gate. It was one of their top five hundred snacks. This seemed to back up Michelle's basic argument.

"We could have those weeds cleared for you in twenty minutes," their munching said.

"I'm not totally confident that they'd distinguish between the amaranth and the squash, though," I said.

"The whole world is breakfast for them," Michelle conceded. "I'm kind of jealous. I mean, they make bark sound delicious."

This was no exaggeration. Natalie actually moaned with pleasure when I dropped a hunk of alfalfa hay into the corral. Myself, I had no such inclination. I'd tried a mouthful of their organic alfalfa out of curiosity, and it tasted like green paper.

"On the other hand," I said. "They don't get to watch Peter Sellers movies."

We probably could have bypassed the whole weed problem if I wasn't so dedicated to organic standards: the Monsanto Corporation, in fact, offers a variety of corn genetically modified to resist a Monsanto poison that will kill everything else in your garden. Just plant, spray, and collect farm subsidies.

> Organic farming can produce enough food to sustain even a larger population than the current worldwide one, without increasing the amount of agricultural land needed.

But the truth is I didn't begrudge a second of garden work. If I couldn't imagine a Fertile Crescent farmer at the dawn of agriculture sharing our particular weed/goat quagmire, I also hoped that any ancient cultivator would have had as much fun not solving his problems as Michelle and I were having not solving ours. There was something about playing in dirt that took us back to some of our more carefree days of varsity preschool: when play was work and you took it seriously. Jeans are meant to have dirty knees, I remembered after a break of three decades.

Meanwhile, despite the prolific weeds, my new apple saplings grew encouraging leaves almost immediately, chard soon came off my grocery store shopping list, and the corn and bean rows in particular really went crazy. I started to get a "this just might work!" feeling. The carbon miles were coming out of my diet by the week. It looked like my supermarket days were numbered.

That is, until the most devastating late-spring hailstorm that anyone can remember sent me back to square one. Ice gob-stoppers pockmarked everyone's truck hoods, and when I skidded home from a fortuitous town run, missing the storm, the river and my creek were both at Nile flood levels, trapping me for about an hour. At the general coffee klatch that ensued while we waited for yet another Old Testament plague to sub-side, Will Ogden's wife told me, "If you had a garden, you don't anymore."

And historians wonder why Jamestown struggled? Those people didn't have co-ops and Wal-Mart to fall back on. The weather patterns for the next couple of millennia, if the *Farmer's Almanac* and local wisdom are to be believed, are best categorized by the description, *"worst drought ever followed by worst flood ever followed by freakiest hailstorm ever followed by some other nightmare, etc."*

Only the squash and a couple of peas survived the deluge without at least some damage. (The peas were already clinging firmly to their mesh wall and the plants were holding hands, a teamwork strategy that no doubt got them through the storm.) I replanted everything as quickly as I could, but the event was the first in a series of frustrating setbacks for me in the food-gathering arena.

Most notably, the Funky Butte Ranch's next two births, the cutest little fluff-ball chicks you ever saw, were scooped up by the red-tailed hawk that nested on the next ranch before they even saw their first weekend, which got me down. Growing up in the suburbs, I just never envisioned myself chasing a bird of prey, screaming, "Hey! Bring those chicks back!" They didn't teach it in precalc.

"She's just trying to feed her family," Michelle reminded me as I bolted for the shotgun.

A few days after that, the second most devastating late-spring hailstorm anyone can remember blitzkrieged across southern New Mexico, this time while Sadie and I were on our run. It was like living in a driving range. Until it happens, you simply don't expect golf balls to pound you on the head while you're on a tour of your neighborhood. This is what Chicken Little was worried about.

We were right in the thick of it, and it got truly scary for a while, with violet lightning missiles dancing on both sides of us, apparently closing in. With each soul-readjusting clap of close-by thunder, Sadie did a couple of mad circles around my legs and then tilted her head up to me quizzically as if to ask, "What do we do now?" Her hair was sticking up as though she were suffering an electric shock, and I almost laughed, until I noticed from my arm hair that the same was true of me. We *were* experiencing an unstable electrical situation.

"Pray," I advised my dog. She was familiar with the concept, as miracles happened in her life with regularity. Take the way beef bones from the local butcher would magically emerge from the freezer now and then. Hallelujah! Sadie's reality was filled with the awesome result of prayer. She knew it couldn't hurt.

About two ridges away from my canyon, I took my own advice and bargained with God, promising that if we survived this one, I'd no longer go out for runs when an obvious prophesy was on its way. As they so often seemed to be these days. I turned off my iPod in case it was a lightning draw, though I kept the headphones on as a partial hail helmet. I fought Sergio Leone winds and forged ahead like some kind of hapless British explorer. And so over the next mile and a half I got to experience the strange phenomenon of overheating and hypothermia in the same hour. It's almost like travel—to Ecuador followed almost immediately by Antarctica.

Flood, hail, slow-arriving contractors. What was next? Locusts? Boils? That storm, needless to say, created even more carnage in the garden. As did the one that followed a few days later. I was thrown into a resentful grumpiness, thinking my whole life plan would be sidetracked by this initial agricultural setback. For a few days I grumbled when I should have been humming, swore when I should have given thanks.

SEVENTEEN

REAPING

REWARDS

On a moist and almost nippy June morning, I re-replanted, but I did it while whining the way farmers throughout the history of agriculture have whined when dealing with the benevolent trickster Mother Nature: with diginity; unless I was alone. I suddenly felt like there were just too many tasks involved in green living. And Bill McKibben made it look so easy. At any given moment, about nine loose ends were looming, lingering, appearing, and reappearing. Say, a broken barn door, or nature behaving like Lindsay Lohan. It was to the point that I had no choice but to implement an "if it's important I'll notice it again" policy when some new problem popped up in front of me as I was treading water on any given day.

After the third storm, Michelle sensed my pending implosion, and suggested we take an afternoon off to innertube the river for summer solstice. But I whined to her that before I could do something like "innertube the river," I had to feed three species of mammal and one of bird, check the house battery bank charge, do some math to make sure the holding tank was full enough for the morning drip watering, scare away any threatening hawks or coyotes, dump a couple of gallons of waste veggie oil into the filter barrel, and maybe do a little emergency goat hoof trimming. All while not getting bitten by a rattlesnake. But *then* I'd be totally free until the evening goat feeding, as long as nothing broke, leaked, or climbed through the pet door and onto my bed (this was Melissa's latest trick).

Unless, of course, it'd been cloudy for a couple of days, in which case I had to do any showering and laundry by the afternoon, to give the pump enough time to fill the holding tank before sundown. Otherwise there'd be no water for breakfast in the morning. The thing about solar power is you need the sun to power it.

> The first solar cell was developed in Bell Labs in 1954. It still generates electricity. Solar panels routinely come with thirty-year warranties.

Life was just more . . . manual than it had been on Long Island when operating the television remote control had been my biggest physical chore. Still, Michelle, Sadie, and I floated the river, and when we returned, the world hadn't ended. In fact, everything was fine at the ranch: goats, solar batteries, water supply.

So I stopped gaping at the sky in dread like Chicken Little as I went through the motions of getting the garden back in order. And like an unsought reward, the monsoon for once came right on schedule to help things along. Within two weeks the garden looked like a weedy Eden again. Plus, I had enough hay stashed in the barn this year to outlast even another epic flood. Organic, New Mexico–grown hay at that. I still planned on trekking to the El Otro Lado river crossing to shoot the breeze with Will Ogden, but this year such coffee klatches would be voluntary.

Even the chickens were recovering—they are blessed with extremely short memories and I'd be hard pressed to say Agatha even remembered her old boyfriend. The hens were back to two eggs per day by August.

"I'm the king of the world!" my new rooster, Donald Trump, loudly boasted as he led his family to a shady pecking spot. "I have eight girlfriends."

"Check that, seven," he crowed the next day after the hawk paid a visit. "Still, who's cooler than me?"

At about that time, weeds once again became the bane of my life. "May this be the worst thing that ever happens to you," my grandmother, who Natalie looks like, used to say to me when I came home weeping with a skinned knee. Indeed, when garden weeds are your biggest problem, life is pretty good.

Michelle and I proceeded to spend much of July avoiding dealing with them. Instead, we kept planting new crops to get weedy when we weren't eating pudding at three a.m. When we finally got to thinning the prickly forest toward the end of the month, we found hidden carrots, leeks, and broccoli that had been protectively shaded by the unwanted "weeds." The brutal New Mexico sun, even at monsoon time, had been tempered by our shrewd laziness to allow the fall harvest to grow to cornucopia levels. On top of that, we found out that amaranth leaves are not just edible, but as nutritious as spinach—our weeds were part of the garden.

"We've got to remember to implement this strict nonweeding regimen next year," I said. "Not before the end of July do we start thinning and grooming."

"I'll mark it down on the calendar," Michelle said between mouthfuls of pudding. "Or we'll forget. We don't want to be late for neglecting the garden."

In truth, I don't know what we did right. Maybe it was beginner's luck, or the wet July. Daily, automated drip irrigation didn't hurt. Michelle not-so-secretly believes it was our Bob Marley song that did the trick, which she sang to the goats (as thanks for their manure) just outside the garden egg fence on the day before the first flowering zucchini looked ready to bear fruit.

It's the Pan Sisters' favorite song, a modified version of "Them Belly Full." It goes like this:

Them belly full but they hungry,
A hungry goat is every goat . . .

The next day a dozen zukes were hanging from the vine. Whatever the source of the bounty, by August I harvested more lettuce than I could reasonably be expected to eat in a year, if I was a rabbit. I stuffed it in gallon bags and put it in the fridge. Peas came next. And like magic one morning there were twenty stir-fries' worth of peppers on the stalk. They were shiny—like earrings from the early Madonna era. I liked looking at them. Michelle stuffed some of them with cream cheese and fried them, and when she dumped the oil from the effort into a mason jar, I thanked her for saving it. "This'll get the ROAT twenty yards, easy."

In mid-August we had some friends over, and ate a dinner comprised of food totally from the Funky Butte Ranch and our valley. Except for tamari. And mushrooms. And, well, beer. But we're working on all three of these things.

Lettuce, tomatoes, sprouts, peas, chard, broccoli, leeks, carrots, rosemary, basil, apples, peaches, eggs—everything was home grown or from neighbors that night. Even the honey on our Mimbres apples came from the next canyon over. And we were still feasting on the appetizers at this point: the corn, beans, and squash were a month away from harvest, though little silk-wrapped cobs were already forming on the cornstalks. Michelle and I started talking about building a greenhouse to cut the carbon miles out of our more tropical limes, avocadoes, and bananas.

> One bushel of corn will sweeten four hundred cans of cola. But the human body has difficulty processing high fructose corn syrup, and many nutritionists see it as a major cause of obesity. Cane sugar is more expensive than corn syrup.

And come next spring, if all went as planned, I would be the valley's ice cream man. My neighbor Pat had got herself a billy goat, which she was willing to lease to me for the necessary twenty minutes next fall. I thought the Pan Sisters could breed by then without stigma. Natalie would kid first. I felt a little like a pimp pairing her off like that, without even the opportunity to date for a while, but this was how it worked in the goat social scene. And I had a goat-milking tutorial visit scheduled in September with Heather, my fairy goatmother neighbor. This is something I'd have to be good at for at least the next two years, once Natalie gave birth. I already had takers for her offspring. Who wouldn't want a Natalie kid?

Next summer I hoped to find myself playing a genuine producer in a consumer society. For most of the world's people, this is pretty much par for the course. It's a matter of survival. For a latchkey kid nurtured on *Gilligan* and Quarter Pounders, it's a sign that truly anything is possible. Like an Exxon executive biking to work. And it only took me thirty-six years.

> Curdled goat milk makes a great base for house paint.

I got the sense my reduction in carbon miles was already significant when one August morning I heard an invisible Michelle say, "We're going to have to get a canner for all these veggies. Especially when the beans are ready." She was weeding somewhere in a head-high cornrow.

"Especially if the flood peaks again," I said. If we couldn't get to town for another forty-three days this coming fall, it was nice to know that the goats wouldn't be the only species unlikely to starve.

We ended the summer overwhelmed with bounty. I mean, how much chard does one ranch need? Michelle kept trying to find recipes that called for excessive numbers of peas, but in the end we seemed always to revert to pudding. I skipped to the garden every afternoon to gather fixin's for the evening salad. It was hard to believe that eight weeks earlier, all seemed lost. The chickens and crops had been decimated, as had my morale. Right there in the garden, I gave a small prayer of thanks that in New Mexico, there is time to replant after carnage. Twice. There is, in fact, time for everything. Including life. Including love.

At least 4.8 acres of agricultural land is needed to maintain an American family of four on mainstream dietary standards. Significantly less land is needed for those on a vegetarian diet.

All I had to do now was chop some winter wood and plant the cold weather crops. In fact, it was with spinach seeds in my hand one September morning that I heard the distant crash up by the house. I looked around me. Wait, where were the Pan Sisters? They were here a minute ago. It was not a good sign if these most social of all creatures weren't checking in every couple of seconds.

I bolted up the hill past the barn with dread in my heart, and ended up collapsing in laughter. Melissa was actually using Natalie's back as a launch pad to get at the last of the roses. No doubt she had plenty of time to practice her routine while my soaked mattress had been in this exact spot. She had flipped a small picnic table in her original assault (that was the crash), and had then evidently tried brute force, judging by the dent in my new, impenetrable metal chicken-wire fencing. Now she was going for Olympic-level gymnastics.

"Nine point five," I said, impressed. "I weighted your score for difficulty."

I was starting the goat ejection process when I realized something: I was happy. Happier than I can ever remember being in my adult life. I had rediscovered a childlike joy in the very real-life endeavor of living green.

I hadn't realized it during the battles with the weather, the contractors' spacey schedules, and the Pan Sisters' rose addiction, but I realized it acutely now: just by attempting to live with a little less oil in my life, I'd already won. It wasn't important whether it hailed or whether the roses bloomed. Whether spiny amaranth (and twelve of its cousins) kept amazingly regenerating in the garden like a hydra, or if my first batch of goat ice cream tasted delicious. (OK, that one mattered.) But mostly the promising turn my life had taken was the result of my decision, quite simply, to try.

As I arched awkwardly over the rosebush fence to smell the last flowers and scoop my goats out (with difficulty—their fat asses were getting almost too big to budge, their horns now genuine weapons), I chuckled at how hard I had fruitlessly fought to keep them from these bushes. With their gentle cud chewing and mischievous sense of humor, the Pan Sisters were teaching me to have the patience to realize that running a ranch and cultivating happiness are both a bit like getting in shape for a big running race, with all the progress, skipped days, setbacks, injuries, and major leaps forward.

That's what I heard in their *Mmbah*s now as they protested their latest, and certainly not last, rosebush eviction. "Eventually it will seem easy." Or at least easier.

I kissed the Pan Sisters as I herded them to their corral penalty box and thanked them for the lesson. And I realized that I didn't regret any of the costs of learning it. Meaning the near-drownings. The purple primer baths. Four hundred hours of pointless rose fencing.

Later that evening, Michelle called me outside as I was writing. She sounded worked up—or maybe she knew she had to holler loudly for me to hear over my solar-powered subwoofer. I grabbed my shotgun, expecting coyotes and a session of tap dancing around imaginary rattlesnakes. But I found her behind the studio, kneeling. "Look at these datura flowers."

I looked, although I just wanted to look at her. She was beautiful in the way that only people truly in touch with the Earth are beautiful. She smelled like the outdoors, even indoors. She said, "Some of them only blossom a single time, for one day, and never again."

I bent down to smell a creeping plant I had dismissed as a weed. It was, as Michelle described it, "the scent of the moon" captured within a lavender-white cone blossom that looked like the horn of a gramophone. And as I came back inside with pollen on my nose, I thought I was lucky to be given more than the one shot a datura blossom got. It had taken me a long time to get to this point. I made so many mistakes just in the past year, that if my life was a basketball game, I would've fouled out.

Living local and green was not an all-or-nothing proposition. Each day I had another chance to make good choices, to move toward a healthy, independent, sustainable life. My first year's effort was just an initial step.

I was going to stay with it. Whether the green fad faded or gas got cheap again. And not just for planetary reasons, but for personal ones. I realized, as the monsoon peaked again, that this time I was flooded in with someone I loved, in what was already our home. My neighbor Sandy was right when she told me that mine was a two-person task, but not because it made the chores easier. Rather because it made life infinitely more joyful. Because it gave that crucial concept of home its depth. It gave me something manageable that I tangibly wanted to nurture into future generations. And I thought that's the greatest good I could do.

Ice cream update: The first batches of Official Funky Butte Ranch Organic, Low Carbon-Mile Goat Ice Cream have been produced and immediately ingested. Juicy details and ice cream recipes can be found at http://www.farewellmysubaru.com.

AFTERWORD

MOTIVATED

While my first year of oil reduction started as a deeply personal experience, I, like most people not living in solitary confinement, realize that climate change is a universal crisis. How can I not? Hardly a day goes by on the ranch without another frightening headline materializing on my computer screen: Eskimos' islands washing away and Antarctic penguins vanishing. I've experienced the warmest year on record in New Mexico. In my electronic equipment alone, it's hard to avoid feeling like part of the problem. The factories, the people, and the cows in this country contribute 25 percent of the world's carbon dioxide, though at these rates, we'll be overtaken by China and India by 2048.

Americans have 1,148 cars per one thousand people. China had nine cars per one thousand people, but its economy is increasing 11 percent per year, and new drivers will be competing for a fixed pool of petroleum. Today American passenger cars account for 10 percent of the world's fossil fuel use.

In response, an entire industry of books predicts, in terrifying detail, a near-future without humans (or at least without society as we know it). James Howard Kunstler, for example, cost me a week's sleep when he wrote in *The Long Emergency*, "the national chain stores will be dead. The supermarkets will not be operating. None of the accustomed large-scale systems we depended on for the goods of daily life will be operating as they did, if at all."

The message I think I'm supposed to take from these apocalyptic tomes was, Might as well have as good a time as possible. Nothing matters. We're all screwed. Steal someone's Ferrari.

But as an inveterate optimist, I've decided to operate on the premise that the doomsday predictors are wrong. They always have been so far—about events like Y2K and the millennium and stuff. Though I did get very, very scared. That's partly because journalists, like hen-pecking school-lunch aides, are often rightly accused of being quick to highlight massive problems and considerably slower to offer solutions. It's all well and good to terrify people by pointing out that the melting of the Greenland ice sheet could take out London and New York, but what could you and I do to keep the giant ice cube floating in the North Atlantic? I figure it's gotta be a worldwide effort. One guy throwing up some solar panels isn't going to reverse climate change.

After attempting to live green for one year on the Funky Butte Ranch, here are the five most important conclusions I've come to:

First, vote for sustainable candidates. In other words, make carbon reduction among your top voting priorities. I'm not a member of any political party (deep down, I cling to my Angry Young Man belief that a two-party system is hardly better than a one-party system, and I believe that a brief glance at lobbyist contribution lists bears this out). So I'm a card-carrying Independent. But the past seven years have shown that there's a time to change the system, and there's a time to make sure that the corrupt idiots who are causing the bulk of the world's environmental problems get booted as far from state and national capitals as possible. I envision sort of the inverse of Karl Rove's plans for a permanent Republican Majority. I see a permanent Sustainable-voting Majority.

This doesn't mean I'm advocating always voting for Democrats. Although that party, which took majority control of both houses of the U.S. Congress in 2006, got off to a good start. One of the first things the House of Representatives did after the Dems took control was to pass a bill canceling the absurd billions in tax breaks for the un-sustainable (and ridiculously profitable) oil companies, and transferring the incentives to sustainable technologies like wind and solar. Such a move would have been unthinkable if the GOP was still in control: they are generally more in bed with Big Oil and its associated industries. True, the Senate failed to act on their side of the bill that would, among other provisions, extend solar tax credits. But it was the GOP Senators who threatened the filibuster that killed the bill.

Still, I recommend against blind party voting. Some rust belt

Democrats fight fuel-efficiency increases for fear of pissing off the flailing Big Three ROAT makers. What goads me even more is that some magazine must have put me on a "progressive" mailing list, resulting in enough "Vote for Hillary" junk mail to clear a medium-sized rainforest. So I recommend finding out which of your local candidates—whether it's for the city council or the U.S. House of Representatives—is serious about sustainability. Really ask the candidates: what do you plan to do to make the U.S. (or our city, or school district) carbon-neutral?

When we're explaining this to any friends still hoodwinked by the fear rhetoric of the old model politicians, I think it's best to frame carbon reduction as a way to build a stronger America. Sacrifice doesn't have to figure into the equation, unless you love your Hummer as much as your children. In their essay "The Death of Environmentalism," authors Michael Shellenberger and Ted Nordhaus make the point that, "Talking about the millions of jobs that will be created by accelerating our transition to a clean energy economy . . . moves the environmental movement away from apocalyptic global warming scenarios that tend to create feelings of helplessness and isolation among would-be supporters." In other words, we can only continue to be a consumer-based, private-enterprise-loving society if our model for success is sustainable. Carbon-reduction is patriotic.

Second, think, every day, about the carbon miles you rack up (or avoid) in your diet. Our food choices account for 3o percent of our carbon emissions. Relocated Hmong refugees in Minneapolis have proven that viable gardens can be planted in sidewalk cracks in federal housing complexes. If penniless hill people can become local eaters in a strange land, surely you and I can in a familiar one. This is possible absolutely anywhere. In Alaska, a Tlingit elder once told me that despite the cold climate, in order to starve in the seafood-rich sub-Arctic ecosystem, "you have to be very, very lazy." There's even a fellow raising chickens on a roof in Brooklyn.

If some of us can't hack more than a small garden due to our overscheduled lives, we *can* demand that our local market stock foods grown not just organically (since most pesticides and fertilizers come from petroleum) but locally. That keeps Chilean apples in Chile. We might discover that we have to eat seasonally (apples are a fall fruit in the Northern Hemisphere), but lo and behold, we'll find that every season has its bounties.

And for every food dilemma, every region has its options. I recently discovered that I don't need cane sugar from the tropics to sweeten my yogurt. Desert agave syrup is a delicious natural sweetener from my area. Likewise, a New Englander can use maple sugar. If every American eats seven meals per week from local sources, Barbara Kingsolver writes in *Animal, Vegetable, Miracle*, the nation would use 1.1 million fewer barrels of oil per week. That would hurt no one but oil refiners and shipping companies. And maybe some orchard corporations in Chile. And the odd cardiologist.

Third, drive on something other than fossil fuels, to help create a viable market for biofuels. Beyond the obvious (and legitimate) do-gooder techniques of carpooling to work and biking once or twice a week, the past year has shown me that driving on an alternative fuel, despite the Kung Pao learning curve I've described in this book, is pretty much a breeze: as long as they plug their nose, no one knows I'm pumping something other than diesel or unleaded into my Ridiculously Oversized American Truck. My Vegetable Oil mechanic, Kevin Forrest, says it takes about four to six months to pay off a Veg-Oil conversion in lower fuel costs.

Now, biofuels aren't a panacea. The science of their use is in its infancy, but I wouldn't buy into the backlash propaganda that tries to convince us that all biofuels lack real efficiency compared to petroleum products. I have to believe that harvesting waste oil is better than churning unleaded. And switchgrass, grapeseed oil, and algae all seem like real possibilities. In reality, I suspect some new biofuel will emerge as the sustainable winner.

Fourth, fight sprawl in your community. Sure, in a busy world it's easier to mollify our consciences by sending checks to large organizations that are trying to save panda bears in China, but the secret to sprawl lies in the reality that most of us remain uninvolved in the well-being of our own backyards. Most people can't name their local county officials; you can bet that developers can. I saw this time and again in covering local government: some horrible development erases an open space, and everybody grumbles and wonders how it happened. We actually have to attend meetings to demand that box stores stay out, and that developers use sustainable building and water supply techniques.

We are responsible for our own backyard. For the Biblically-inclined, this mandate reverberates loudly in Ezekiel: "Is it not enough for you to drink clear water? Must you also muddy the rest with your feet?" We can insist on legitimate green certification in all commercial and residential structures in our communities, the way we'll hopefully demand locally-grown and fair trade food at the market. I don't know why this sounds so radical to some ears. Europe is a decade ahead of the U.S. in this area. Holland is running trains on vegetable oil, and all new buildings in Spain already have to meet solar power standards. As for water efficiency, Israel thrives in a desert.

We'll know we have a handle on sprawl when new home sales are no longer reported as a major sector of the American economy. Economists will have to establish a new category to track growth, maybe one that looks at sales of retrofitted pre-existing homes (and businesses) designed in communities that don't require cars to acquire basic necessities. Maybe the category can be called green-home sales.

Fifth, stay atop new carbon-reducing technologies. The world moves too fast in the digital age to rely on one fixed solution. Kevin Forrest points out that my carbon-neutral truck, for example, might just be a temporary solution until hydrogen cells (or some new energy technology) becomes viable. If we hear about a legitimate new green development (like the solar-powered airplane that recently flew for fifty-four straight hours over New Mexico), we can e-mail it to a hundred friends. Thus we can create market demand.

Bill Clinton may not be the savior that Al Gore is when it comes to climate change prognostication, but Clinton is convinced, in his latest book, *Giving*, that smart business decisions by corporations, and savvy and kind behavior by citizens, can solve not just the world's poverty problems, but its ecological ones as well. "By simply changing our buying habits as ordinary citizens," Clinton writes, ". . . the increased demand will cause . . . companies to follow suit."

Indeed, Équiterre is an organization founded on the premise that our wallet is the greatest activist (http://www.equiterre.org/en/). And, believe me, CEOs are paying attention. They might not act until a low-carbon product or behavior is profitable, but it is you and I who can make it so. Number crunchers are standing by to count the dollars we generate.

So buy the Seventh Generation toilet paper and Earth-friendly dish soap. I like the "think about seven generations from now" motif in Native American mythology and I try to incorporate it, plus a little Hindu meditation and Buddhist worldview, into my Judaism. And I appreciate it when anyone gives a noble idea the ol' college try, even when it's rife with a little consumer hypocrisy. It's better than lying to start a war so you can enrich the vice president's company.

By far the greatest impact we can have on crafting a sustainable future is not just by buying "green products," but rather by actively understanding that every part of life can and should be infused with carbon reduction. It's not just about oil prices and organic produce. When we, say, pay our garbage bill, we can make our voices heard about where the waste goes (by calling our local town or country representative and attending waste board meetings. Dick Gephardt once said that the U.S. is not a representative democracy; it's a representative democracy of those who participate).

We've got every right to ask, "Is everything possible being recycled?" "Is the methane from the landfill harvested for power?" We're the ones paying the sanitation contractor. The same goes with public sewer service: the technology exists today for municipal waste effluent to leave the processing plant as potable water and compost. Yet oftentimes, decades-old technologies dump raw or nearly raw waste into rivers and oceans. There is no reason for this, other than inertia.

We also need to think about where our grid power comes from. We can call our electric company, enjoy the Muzak while we spend an hour wading through the voice mail system in search of a human, and when we finally get through, we can find out if the generating station for our home area is powered by coal, nuclear energy, or natural gas (mine uses all three), and ask what the plans are to move to cleaner options. Some grid companies are already shifting to sustainable options like wind or solar. These utilities give us the option of paying more to offset the cost of their not killing us. If our electric company is not going green, we can cease to be customers, and use the wind or the sun to power our homes on our own (this isn't so easy for people living in an urban apartment, but even these folks can lobby their congressperson to change utility rules or convince their building manager to take the whole structure solar). Take it from me, it's an investment, but it will drastically reduce your fossil fuel footprint and give you energy independence, should anything happen to utility grid power. Once you buy the equipment, "the sun's free," as Herbie the solar guru likes to say. Though Rupert Murdoch is said to be shopping.

Waste and electricity are part of the hidden infrastructure of our lives that we once took for granted. We need to train ourselves to immediately have awareness of our global impact in all aspects of life. For example, if we switch our homes to solar power, we can make noise about the packaging the panels are stuffed into if it is not recycled. It's our money and we can take it wherever we like. We can ask our dentist where the enamel comes from. We can ask our bank to use a kinder material than vinyl for checkbook covers, and we can demand that the department store's landscaping is local and sustainable. We can and should be pains in the ass about this stuff until a carbon-reduced mind-set is as mainstream as a Kenny G solo. And we can make sure our friends care (and vote), too.

Eventually we really will find that living sustainably and thinking about our carbon footprint permeates every part of our day: the paper in our printer, the material in our decking, our children's cafeteria lunch food—is it organic and local? I say we should think big. Shoot, why *can't* our air fleet move to solar? Why can't the state or local government transfer federal highway funds toward rebuilding a decrepit or non-existent public transportation system? I see it as a new civil rights movement. Every corner of our society has to be infused with a move toward low-carbon emissions and overall non-sprawl sustainability, the way that every business decision today, by moral and codified law, has to be conducted without bias as to race. When it comes to infusing sustainability society-wide, in 2008 we're still in the age of Jim Crow.

A fair number of brainwashed people still think that environmentalists are hurting the economy, the same way some said integration would damage American culture. A critical mass of folks is only now starting to realize that sustainable life is the only way to survive as a society. I like to imagine looking back in forty years and having President Winfrey (or, if you like, President Kid Rock or President Nugent) humbly remember a time when we were actually shortsighted enough to pollute our own atmosphere to the point that we almost couldn't live in it anymore. It will seem laughable. I hope.

These five steps can be taken together or piecemeal. I have to admit, even the first item on this list of suggestions (installing carbon-reducing politicians) is proving a tricky one for me. Here I am preaching sustainability, and my own U.S. representative doesn't have a basic understanding of the importance of predator/prey balance in our vast New Mexican ecosystem (he wants to exterminate all wolves). Resisting the urge to be conspiratorial about backroom gerrymandering in my state, I'll lay it on myself and likeminded community members to raise enough awareness to get this nineteenth-century joker out of office and replace him with someone wiser than an eight-year-old.

Which actually leads to a sixth suggestion that overlays all the previous five. I think it's the most important one of the bunch. We should, we *must*, infuse the next generation with an under-standing about sustainable living in our intertwined world. In the course of everyday life, we've got to let our kids know that things will soon be changing (hopefully for the better) in all of the basic elements of our lives. Part of every education should include lessons in where our food, clothing, water, transporta-tion, and fuel comes from. Better yet, we can trash the Game Boys and teach kids how to provide all of the above without fos-sil fuels or exploitation. For many of us this will mean learning right alongside our whippersnappers. That's what Google is for.

The obstacles to crafting a sustainable society sound formi-dable. We live in a massive nation going through one of its most corrupt, violent periods (someday, the 2000 and 2004 U.S. election frauds will illustrate how primitive the U.S. represen-tative democracy was in its first three hundred years), but in society, as in physics, disorder often precedes positive change.

I see with my own eyes how the six suggestions I've laid out here *actually work in the real world* on the local level. In my community, townies in Silver City with full-time jobs have formed a goat co-op, where a dozen families share their milk, greatly reducing the time commitment necessary for providing healthy, local, carbon-free protein. And this in a highly populated, growing town.

Even closer to home, in my own rural valley, local apple farmers were almost out of business a few years ago because the supermarket chains were buying only from the monoculture producers who, according to my orchard-tending neighbor Davey Menendez, guaranteed that "you'll never see a worm or a brown spot." Well, one of my valley friends helped start a local farmer's market and a harvest festival featuring some of the most tasty apples I've every crunched. And I've already mentioned the valley co-op that saves all of us from driving fifty roundtrip miles to town every time we need a carrot. This market (coyotes permitting) features my eggs, as well as local vegetables and organic, sustainably-raised valley beef. These institutions are the real reasons I can go days without starting my truck: living in a functioning community economy, I don't always need to start an engine to lead a modern, comfortable life.

We all lead busy lives, and so I don't think we have to make all these changes at once in order to be a good carbon citizen. And we don't have to grow all our own food in order to eat locally. We don't even have to build our own furniture in order to shop locally. In fact, there is a long precedent for dividing labor in indigenous communities that predates box stores. I recall something a Tlingit canoe carver once told me in coastal Alaska. I was marveling at all the indigenous skills I didn't possess, wondering how I ever would have survived before, say, FedEx and Thai takeout.

"You know, there was always trade," he said. "We carved, and the folks farther north rendered the fish oil. Not everybody had to know how to do everything." This mind-blowing fact of vibrant, segmented, pre-Western economics helped me live at peace with the reality that I couldn't personally perform every task necessary to live sustainably. But I can try to get most of what I need close to home. I want to send as many Chinese factory slaves back to the countryside as I can. Even Kunstler writes in the usually apocalyptic *Long Emergency*, "life . . . will be intensely local and success or failure will depend on the quality of each community."

Even though scientists and doomsday authors might disagree about our prospects, I believe strongly in the interconnectedness of all things, and so, in the end, my oil-reduction efforts come back to the personal. It's about more than just my carbon footprint. If I take steps that feel like positive ones for the Earth and my community, then I am taking positive steps for myself.

GREEN TIDBITS
TO CHEW ON

---

1. Batteries are the big ugly hole in a solar-powered life. Not only are the dozen golf cart–sized batteries that store the sun's energy for me at the ranch immensely heavy—they easily weigh seventy pounds each—but they are an environmental nightmare. Contradiction city. The lead inside them is responsible for defiling much of Canada. During my solar installation, every time I herniated my back by hauling one to my leaky power center behind the laundry room, I coated my hands with a tasty dusting of sulfuric acid, just in time for lunch. Yum. Plus, these batteries last for only ten years, max, which then becomes a landfill issue.

Johnny Weiss, co-founder and executive director of Solar Energy International, an educational nonprofit (www.solarenergy.org), told me not to hold my breath for improvements. "For the most part, we're using the same battery technology that Thomas Edison used with our space-age solar panels." Presently, an Austin-based company called EEStor is getting a lot of publicity with its supposedly revolutionary super-battery because of financing from big-time venture capitalists, but we'll see: the alternative energy world is full of "next greatest thing" technologies that never seem to make it into my solar supply catalogue. At least not yet.

2. Lately, the cost of solar components has been rising about 10 percent a year because of the dang demand in energy-efficient Europe and because the world's supply of the silicon that goes into solar panels is limited. I bought four solar panels in anticipation of getting off the grid. Then it took me a year to get all the necessary components and roust the local contractors. Once I met with my solar electrician, I learned that I needed four more panels of the same 165-watt size. These four cost about a hundred dollars more each than the first four. I blame Vladimir Putin. He's scaring Europe so badly with his threats to switch off the Russian natural gas taps that it's turning soccer hooligans into environmentalists.

3. Sometimes having a "grid inter-tie" system, that is, a solar- or wind-power setup that is still connected to the energy company's power lines, can be even more effective than moving off the grid entirely. In many states, utilities are required to buy back any surplus energy you produce with your home solar panels or wind generator. Instead of receiving an electric bill, you can receive an electric check.

4. Store your alternative fuels away from the house. Recently, I woke to a dog pack covered in vegetable oil, as Michelle's two hounds and Sadie, now one happy family at the Funky Butte Ranch, got into a wrestling match right where I had stored the batch of waste oil that I had collected from Sisters Restaurant the previous day. The dogs, who made the house smell like moldy manicotti for several weeks, had shiny, oily coats for at least that long. And so I learned that if you're going to collect your own gas, you need to set aside some space for your own gas station. Hope-fully, the coating of flammable oil that now rings my house will evaporate before it might set the ranch ablaze like a tinderbox.

5. You cannot train a goat to sit, stay, or roll over, though with persistent training you can get one to yodel the first verse of "Them Belly Full."

RESOURCES

www.farewellmysubaru.com—The adventure doesn't stop here. Stay up to date on goings on at the Funky Butte Ranch and discuss the issues raised in this book.

www.abqaltenergies.com—Website for Albuquerque Alternative Energies.

www.solar-nation.org—An alternative energy political activist organization.

www.solarenergy.org—Solar Energy International, an educational nonprofit that holds wind and solar workshops.

www.localharvest.org/csa—A website for finding sources of Community Supported Agriculture (CSA) anywhere in the continental United States. CSA is a partnership in which you, the produce eater, help cover the costs of a local farm, in return for getting a regular delivery of seasonal local fruits and veggies.

www.cspinet.org—Center for Science in the Public Interest is a health, food and consumer safety, and scientific organization, that, among other things, can tell you how much saturated fat is in your enchiladas.

www.vegoil.us—National VegOil Board, a nonprofit research, educational, and promotional group dedicated to using grease as a fuel.

www.treehugger.com—A media outlet "dedicated to driving sustainability mainstream."

www.foe.org/globalbiofuelsdatabase—An environmental group's database concerned with the ecological impact of different kinds of biofuels.

www.dripworks.com—A company that sells efficient drip-irrigation systems.

www.campaignearth.org—A website that provides monthly steps that can be taken to reduce carbon emissions.

www.grist.org—Everything from green politics to green humor to a green job board. You'll come out looking like Kermit the Frig.

www.off-grid.net—Anecdotal and practical articles about anything off the grid.

www.fillup4free.com—Need a vegetable oil fill-up in Cleveland? Might want to give a look here.

www.plentymag.com—Proving green can be fun, in *Plenty* magazine you'll find green dentists, green gear, and even investigations into why local food movements are allegedly being stifled.

www.consumerenergycenter.org/cgi-bin/eligible_pvmodules
.cgi—The State of California publishes solar panel efficiency
ratings for just about every panel on the market, which you can
find right here.

www.dsireusa.org—A website that lists solar tax incentives on
the individual state level.

www.energytaxincentives.org—A website that follows the latest
on the developing debate on federal tax subsidies.

www.envirotech.blogspot.com—A strong resource for anybody
serious about walking the green walk, from which fish species
are overfished to the latest on the world CO_2 situation.